UNDERCOVER
Angel

Norma Strang

First published by Ultimate World Publishing 2020
Copyright © 2020 Norma Strang

ISBN

Paperback - 978-1-922372-84-0
Ebook: 978-1-922372-85-7

Norma Strang, has asserted her right under the Copyright, Designs and Patents Act 1988 to be identified as the author of this work. The information in this book is based on the author's experiences and opinions. The publisher specifically disclaims responsibility for any adverse consequences, which may result from use of the information contained herein. Permission to use information has been sought by the author. Any breaches will be rectified in further editions of the book.

All rights reserved. No part of this publication may be reproduced, stored in or introduced into a retrieval system, or transmitted in any form, or by any means (electronic, mechanical, photocopying, recording or otherwise) without the prior written permission of the author. Any person who does any unauthorised act in relation to this publication may be liable to criminal prosecution and civil claims for damages. Enquiries should be made through the publisher.

Cover design: Patti Roberts
Layout and typesetting: Ultimate World Publishing
Editor: Anita Saunders
Graphics: angel with sword #105205779 © bogadeva1983
woman #173808352 © kharchenkoirina

Ultimate World Publishing
Diamond Creek,
Victoria Australia 3089
www.writeabook.com.au

This book is based on my personal life journey and is written from my own memories, feelings and perspective on the events described. I have made every attempt to be respectful and thoughtful in my writings of these events, and for those people who feature in my story. Some of the names have been changed. I am aware that they will have their own memories, feelings and perspective on these times and events, and only tell my own story within these pages.

Dedication

For my Hamish, an angel in fur, who stood steadfastly beside me through the most challenging times in my life and who left a legacy for many human and animal souls, whose suffering is now eased by the healing plant he guided me to. He and his unconditional love were my reasons for being.

For my Bhride Baggins, an angel in fur who chose to stay down here with me a while longer, for which I am most grateful. Her strength, enormous heart, quirky sense of fun and deepest love have brought much love, laughter and joy to my life.

For Mark, who made me laugh again. And whose love, respect and support for me and what I do helped me heal deep wounds.

For all the undercover angels waiting to remember, this is for you.

Contents

Dedication	v
Foreword	ix
Chapter One: A Life-Changing Diagnosis	1
Chapter Two: The Gift of Bikram Yoga	11
Chapter Three: Warning From an Elder	21
Chapter Four: The Pinnacle of Happiness	29
Chapter Five: The Bubble Bursts	41
Chapter Six: Betrayal	49
Chapter Seven: India	55
Chapter Eight: Visit From a Friend	67
Chapter Nine: New Boyfriend	79
Chapter Ten: Malignant Love	91
Chapter Eleven: Empath and Narcissist	101
Chapter Twelve: The Dismantling	115
Chapter Thirteen: Bikram's Fall Off the Pedestal	125
Chapter Fourteen: Final Goodbyes	139
Chapter Fifteen: My Angels	151
Chapter Sixteen: Promise to a Dog	163
Chapter Seventeen: Return to Love and Purpose	173

Foreword

"Each of us is a book waiting to be written, and that book, if written, results in a person explained."
             Thomas M. Cirignano

I am not a writer, but I have a story to tell. One that may help you through these challenging times. This is the account of a portion of my life which led me to live in isolation for years.

What got me there? No, it was not a virus, or a lockdown. It was my own choice to live that way after a period of extreme loss, betrayal and heartbreak. The reason I have decided to share such personal information with you, dear reader, is that in that place, I remembered who I was and what I came to do here. I look around today and see the whole world in the place that I once was. How did I cope? What did I do? How did I survive through the loneliness, despair, lack of love and finances, and continued blows to my spirit that brought me to my knees, over and over?

How did I get back up? And who have I become because of that period in my life?

I invite you to meet the person I was and the person I became. To witness how I evolved through depression and feeling displaced into a self-aware, empowered human being. If you have forgotten who you are or why you came to this earth, I pray you will awaken and rise like the phoenix to be the person you were born to be.

In the cocoon the caterpillar literally dies and 'imaginal' cells create the butterfly. It goes through its metamorphosis in pain and alone. It is in the darkness we can find the light and in solitude we can find the Self.

This is my metamorphosis.

CHAPTER ONE

A Life-Changing Diagnosis

"There are wounds that never show on the body that are deeper and more hurtful than anything that bleeds."
Laurell K. Hamilton

"You have depression," the doctor said.

It was a doctor I had never seen before. He wasn't very friendly. He wasn't very warm, but he managed to work out that I had depression, even though I omitted to tell him that only days prior I had been in hospital after a near-fatal overdose. The only reason I had visited the doctor was because I had taken a week off work after the attempted suicide and I needed to obtain a letter to give to my employer, so he knew that I wasn't just slacking off. I had no intention of listening to anything the doctor said, and I certainly wasn't about to take antidepressants, but I knew that my life really needed to change. This wasn't the first attempt at suicide. The last one was when I was about to turn 30 years old, a week before my birthday.

The doctors did not know how I even survived the previous attempt, and told me that they had never seen anyone on record survive such an overdose, and here it was, happening again.

My manager wasn't there the day I walked into the *Herald Sun* where I was running the Cars-Guide, but the assistant manager was, so I pulled out the letter and handed it to him.

"Hey, Brian, I, um, I um, I … well, I have depression," I stuttered.

I was so embarrassed and ashamed to say these words, and this was probably the reason why I had never really told anyone before. And just to add to the shame that I felt, he replied, "Really? I never thought YOU would be the type of person to get depression."

I wished the floor could have swallowed me up. I felt humiliated, embarrassed and ashamed. It was one of the hardest things I've ever had to speak out loud and I wished I'd never told him. But I had told him. In fact, I felt so vulnerable, I immediately made my mind up not to tell my manager or anyone else.

So I did what probably most people do when they have a serious diagnosis that is not taken seriously or understood in our society, and that's play it down. Maybe I just needed a week off, I told myself; I'm just tired, perhaps I'm working too late. Any excuse but face the truth. However, I knew in my heart that I had reached a crucial turning point. If I was meant to leave this planet, I would have been well gone. But what direction to go in? By conventional standards, I had everything. The successful job, plenty of money, living in a beautiful waterfront apartment. I was attractive, slim, the life of the party. I had achieved something within my position that I was told initially couldn't be achieved. The company said they would have been happy if I could just maintain the amount of income that my department generated. In fact, they said it probably couldn't have been improved upon. One of the key factors of producing such a high income was that I managed to encourage the advertisers to pay for colour advertisements, which up until that point was thought impossible. They told me the sales team were pretty good but I decided otherwise; within a year, I had sacked 70% of them.

I wasn't the most popular person in the building, largely because of the amount of time I spent in Human Resources firing people.

"It's the way you speak to them, Norma. They don't like it," I was told.

"I'm Scottish," I explained. A glaringly obvious fact, bearing in mind I had one of the strongest Scottish accents you could imagine!

"We even shout when we say I love you," I emphasised.

The long and short of it was, I brought in and trained a whole new sales team which abruptly turned the entire department around. I had pretty much done everything that I could do in this role and the general consensus was that I would be promoted. Success on the corporate ladder was assured, including an ever-increasing income and considerable status and recognition. Not to mention a bigger apartment, or another house. Another flashy car. I was already driving a hot little sports car. I had all the clothes any woman could want. I travelled overseas, taking my clients on five-star trips and enjoying the benefits of that myself. My clients loved me and that feeling was reciprocated; it was one of the highlights of my job.

This was success, wasn't it? Or was it? Why was I so unhappy? Why was I so unhappy that I had done something so drastic as attempt to end my life? It was a hard enough question to ask, let alone answer.

It has to be the job, I reasoned. So, I started to search for other options. I joined an agency and asked them to look for another position for me. They created a very impressive CV, and I was very specific about the income I wanted to earn.

That's it, I thought. I'll just change my job. That's what it is. I've done this for two years and achieved everything I possibly could. I need something new.

I did seem to want to change every two years. In fact, my previous employer had perceptively remarked to me, "Norma, you need change every two years. You're great at setting things up."

He was right. I knew myself well enough to know that I thrived on creating and developing. He was pretty smart, though. He knew how to recognise a good employee and he knew how to take care of them. Every two years I would go to him and say, "John, I'm going to leave. I need to find something else." Whereupon he would pull me into the boardroom and say, "Let's have a look at what else you could do."

And before I knew it, I would be developing one of his many ideas into a successful business. He was intuitive enough to know what I needed to remain inspired and motivated and because of this, I worked with him for 10 years.

Shortly after I made the decision to find another job, the phone rang one evening.

"Norma, we have an interview lined up for you," announced the girl from the agency, who was job hunting on my behalf.

"Wonderful!" I exclaimed. "Tell me about it?"

A Life-Changing Diagnosis

"They are looking for someone to manage seven automobile magazines, Australia wide. They have looked at your CV and are impressed with your ability to be able to cohesively organise a department and cut away any dead wood," she explained.

As she described the nature of the job, I instantly had a sinking feeling. Obviously, they wanted a hatchet man to do exactly what I had done with the sales team at the *Herald Sun*. I had been hoping to explore something with less visits to the Human Resources department.

Nevertheless, I went along for the interview. I knew that I could do the job standing on my head, on top of which, the salary was nearly double what I was currently earning.

A couple of days later, the agency called again.

"Norma, we just want to ask you a question. It looks like you're going to get the position. If they offer it to you, what will your answer be?"

"Yes," I heard myself reply.

It was the strangest feeling; it was almost as if my response was not far short of a knee-jerk reaction. I simultaneously felt my stomach do a massive somersault. A sensation that I was later to realise was my own internal warning system.

After I hung up the phone, I walked into the bathroom, and looked in the bewildered reflection of myself in the mirror.

"What the fuck is wrong with you?" I said out loud.

Deep down, I knew that I didn't really want this job and that it wasn't going to make any difference to the state of my wellbeing.

I began negotiations with the girl in the mirror.

"Right," I said. "If I'm supposed to get this job, if it's going to make me happy, if it's going to change things, I will take it, and I'll give it 150%. But if I'm not supposed to get it, if it's not going to make me happy, if it's not going to change where I'm at, please don't let me get this job, and I promise I will go home to my family in Scotland and spend some time there instead."

Well, the universe must've heard me, because the next day at lunch I got a phone call from the agency.

"Norma, I have some news for you."

The tone of her voice was distinctly different to the optimism in her previous phone calls. She sounded like she was about to break some very bad news, but was hesitant to do so.

"I'm, well, I'm just … um…" she stumbled. "I'm really sorry to tell you, but out of nowhere this guy showed up with all this internet experience, and they've decided they want to go with him."

"Yes!" I shouted, almost surprising myself at the intensity of my response.

"Oh, are you okay?" she said. "I didn't really expect that kind of reaction. I thought you would be really disappointed; you seemed to be very keen on the job."

"No, no, it's okay," I reassured her. "I've just made a promise to myself about what I really need, and this is just confirmation. Thank you so much for all your help. You've no idea how much you've helped me."

I hung up the phone and walked back to my sales team at the lunch table.

"What are you so happy about?" one of my team members asked.

A Life-Changing Diagnosis

"I'm just about to resign," I said, with the biggest smile on my face.

My next task was to hand in my resignation. My manager scratched his head in confusion. It was a remarkable turn of events. After all, it was only months before that I had been the star of the *Herald Sun* awards night, where most of the evening I was on stage, handing out awards to my team. It was a big event. I always thought of it as the Oscars of the media world.

"You really want to resign now?" he asked, wide-eyed. "You're just about to receive enormous commissions for all your hard work."

"I know it sounds completely nuts; it's just not fulfilling anymore, so I've decided to move back to Scotland and spend some time with my family."

Before I knew it, I was packing up my very neat apartment, putting everything in storage and heading back to my homeland. It had been 17 years since I arrived in Australia and it really had been a struggle for me not having any family. In my mind, going back to my roots and being with family again could possibly be the answer.

I arrived back into the familiar surrounds of Scotland in the bleak mid-winter. Walking out of the arrivals lounge at Edinburgh Airport I pulled my coat close around me and took a sharp inhale of breath as the cold air flooded me with memories of my younger years. I gazed out of the car window looking at the familiar Scottish landscape, the grey mists rolling over the countryside and the distant snow-capped hills. Even after all these years, it still felt like coming home.

My mum was so excited to see me home. She embraced me with a brief Scottish bear hug. It has to be said that the Scots were never big on overt expressions of emotions, or hugging, for that matter!

I had this picture in my head about how wonderful it was going to be. Me and my family again, and my school friends. Yet as life so often proves, it was not to be the fairy tale I imagined.

Within a few days I was struggling with the food. The Scottish diet was a world away from the diet I had been used to. It was as if the Scots were still eating the heavy food that was required in the bleakest winters to warm the body, even though the winters were much milder. The mention of haggis was enough to traumatise any vegetarian. Haggis—a combination of animal offal cooked inside a sheep's stomach. Who on earth thought of such a thing? I was a vegetarian, which seemed to baffle the restaurant staff.

"Oh, you're a vegetarian," one waitress said to me on an evening out with my younger brother and his family.

"That's no problem," she proudly beamed. "We have chicken!"

"Well, that is a dead bird," I laughed. "Not quite vegetarian; do you have anything that has not been killed?"

"Oh, I see," she said, wide-eyed, and thought for a minute. "What about mushroom risotto?" she asked.

"That will do nicely," I winked with a smile.

Mushroom risotto or grilled mushrooms seemed to be the only options on the Scottish menus for vegetarians. Catching up with my friends seemed to always include drinking alcohol. In my younger years I had been the biggest party girl of them all, consuming whisky like soft drink. I had recently started yoga and just wasn't drinking so much alcohol anymore. I was really missing the natural high that came from doing my yoga. Before I knew it, I was on the internet trying to find somewhere to do yoga and meditate. Then I would know what to do.

A Life-Changing Diagnosis

One evening I walked into the lounge room where my mother was watching TV. I must've looked lost again.

"Are you seeing your friends then?" she asked.

"No, Mum," I said with a sad face. "They've got their own lives now. They're all married, with children." I was feeling a bit sorry for myself.

"Do you think, Norma, you would have been happier if you had a life like Alison ?" Alison was a friend who seemed to have everything.

"God, NO, Mum," I exclaimed. "Staying here all my life and doing the same thing with the same person all my life would drive me nuts!"

"You know, darling," she said. "I really would love you to stay home. It's been a long time since you've been home. But I'm going to be honest with you. I don't think you'd be happier living back here. Your life is different now, Norma. You're healthy. You eat a lot of different food to your friends and to us. Your life has been outdoors in the sunshine. Your whole lifestyle is different. When you think of it, Norma, your adult life has really been in Australia. You grew up in Australia. I think, my darling, you're more Australian than you know. You don't sound it. You've still got your Scottish accent, but I think you're more Australian than you know."

"You know, Mum, you could be right," I sighed, and got back on the internet trying to find ashrams in India to escape to.

I had meditated for many years and it was part of my daily routine, but I was really missing the physical yoga that had made me feel so good; in fact, that was the reason I had cut down on drinking, even when I was socialising. And that was the reason, probably, that made me aware enough or clear-minded enough to leave the job that I thought was making me unhappy.

I thought, well, if I'm going to do yoga in India, I might as well do the yoga I have been doing in Melbourne. In fact, I might as well go to the teacher training and just do that yoga for nine weeks. Then I'll know what to do. Then I'll have a clear mind. Of course, I had no intention of becoming a teacher. I just wanted to do yoga for nine weeks to work out what the next part of my journey was.

Before I knew it, I was organising to fly to LA to do the nine-week yoga teacher training. Two days before I left, I received a package in the mail. It was the Bikram yoga dialogue, and because I had no intention of becoming a teacher, I had no intention of learning it either. Boy, was that a mistake.

CHAPTER TWO

The Gift of Bikram Yoga

"Every new beginning comes from some other beginning's end."
Seneca

The registration room was filled with fresh-faced, determined yogis and yoginis, who wanted to learn how to teach the yoga that had most probably already changed their own lives.

People were rushing around, getting their room numbers, filling in forms. I was standing still in the middle of the room, when this little Indian man walked past me. He stopped dead in his tracks and said, "I know you. I recognise you. I have met you before," then continued on his way without me having a chance to say a word. That was the very first time I met my teacher, Bikram.

Undercover Angel

"How's your dialogue?" one of my roommates asked me.

"Oh, I only just received it a couple of days before I left, so I don't know it at all," I replied.

I had no idea that this dialogue would become so important in my life. Students were practising their dialogue every spare minute of the day, in between classes, in the toilets, walking up and down the carpark.

The reason they were all so worried is that they had to read the first posture to Bikram. Shit, I thought, as I listened to the umpteenth person reciting their word-for-word perfect dialogue. I sat at the back of a huge line of people, somehow hoping to have miraculously learned it by the time it was my turn to show myself to Bikram.

Bikram was bluntly honest with people. If their voice was monotone, he'd say, "You're boring. You make me want to sleep, not do yoga."

If they were good, he had no problem telling them that too. My heart started to palpitate. Even though I'd no intention of becoming a teacher, I was terrified of public speaking, especially when I did not know one word of what I was supposed to know verbatim.

"Sorry, Bikram," I said as I nervously stood in front of the class of a hundred people. "I only received this a few days ago and I don't know it."

"Then read it," he said. "Someone get her the dialogue."

I had arrived in LA straight from Scotland, and my accent was pretty strong. Imagine, I'm reading the dialogue that an Indian wrote, with a lot of broken English, in a broad Scottish accent, not knowing it at all.

When I finished reading, you could have heard a pin drop. For sure, I was going to get the bad feedback. He held his chin in his hand, cocked his head to the side and said, "Ha, you just wait and see how good YOU'RE going to be!"

Of course, I thought he was mad, because I wasn't even going to be a teacher.

I spent most of the training being one of the worst in the class of a hundred at my dialogue. Every posture, I'd be in the toilet with diarrhoea and doing tapping (the emotional freedom technique) at the same time to try and reduce my nerves.

Bikram was like a celebrity, strutting into the room, looking for attention with his new leopard-print shorts. He was hysterically funny, and seemed to read people at a level way beyond the physical. He said what everybody else was thinking. Sometimes it sounded harsh, other times he was so gentle and caring.

Not everyone adored him. Some didn't like him at all. But in my training, there were few who felt like this. Some were very sycophantic, which to me, coming from Scotland, was cringeworthy behaviour. The anatomy lectures were long, and the pressure was on, because if we didn't pass those exams, we didn't pass the course.

The best class was the 5:00 p.m. class with Bikram. I just loved those classes and watching him in action. There was no doubt in my mind that this man was a true yogi. He was so passionate about the yoga and spreading it to the world, as his guru reportedly requested. I loved hearing him talk about his guru and India.

One evening, he asked for someone to give his shoulders a massage. I lowered my eyes, as I was a qualified masseuse, but did not want to massage Bikram.

"Where are all the massage therapists from the registration forms?" one of the staff shouted.

Silence filled the room. Then one of the admin people said, "Norma, aren't you a masseuse?"

"Oh, yes," I said, "but I've not been doing it for a while."

"That's not a problem. You'll be fine," Bikram said as he waved his hand for me to come over. He was sitting at the front of the room, facing the podium where our evening lecture was taking place. I was ushered to sit behind Bikram where I reluctantly started to massage his shoulders. I was cringing inside. I felt so embarrassed.

I had been doing massage for years in between my corporate jobs. One of the reasons I was not doing much massage anymore was because I seemed to absorb so much from my clients. I had given it up a few years prior when I would come home feeling my clients' ailments. They would come in with a headache and leave feeling amazing. I would have their headache.

Sometimes I would see the student in my mind's eye as a child, and I was able to see where their pain came from. Other times I would feel incredibly sad for hours after the massage.

I remember watching the movie *The Green Mile*. And when Big John took on all the pain from others, then blew it out of his mouth, I would say, "That's what I do, but I don't know how to blow it out."

I was soon to find out more about this 'gift', or 'curse', as I mostly felt it was, why I was able to do this and the consequences of not letting it out.

So here I was, massaging Bikram, and it started. I could see him as a child with his guru, and felt the terrible pain that was deep inside him. It was so strong; I was getting nauseous. After about 15 minutes, I was praying for him to say that's enough, but it went on.

The Gift of Bikram Yoga

Finally, he said, "That's enough, now brush my hair," as he handed me the brush.

I looked around the room, pleading with all the women's eyes who wished they were in my place and said, "Oh, maybe someone else would like a turn."

"No, you do it," Bikram commanded.

I felt myself sinking inside, as if to hide. But someone begged him if she could do it and took over grooming the guru.

Not long after our break, we were awaiting our evening lecture, which normally would go well into the wee small hours. Bikram came into the room and announced that he was tired and going home. Yells of delight filled the room, as we were only too happy to have the night off before 2:00 a.m.

The next day, Bikram came in and told us that he had slept for five hours, which he apparently had not done for years. I smiled, as I heard that so many times before from my clients after having a massage with me.

The training was gruesome, but somehow, I fell in love with the yoga. Even more so at the very last posture. That's when I decided I wanted to be a teacher.

On our last class with Bikram, it was just amazing. He had some energy, that little man. His presence and energy filled and lifted the room. He finished by saying, "Congratulations, teachers." I could not believe the emotion that welled up within me. I had tears of joy pouring down my face; my life was about to change forever.

I arrived back in Scotland the fittest I'd ever been. My body was like a 20-year-old, even though I was reaching 40. I decided to do a tour of

Scotland. Having lived in Australia for 17 years, I didn't even know my own country, so I was very excited about a little trip around Scotland.

I hired a car and headed off towards Findhorn, much to the dread of my mum, who was worried about me going alone. I reminded her that I lived on the opposite side of the world alone, and had travelled extensively alone. I suppose she'd never really seen me heading off on a journey before, so I assured her I was happy to be going alone.

People have no idea of the joy and freedom it brings to travel alone. You can do exactly what you want, with no one to please and no one to answer to. And I had always met amazing people in my travels. I found a cute little bed and breakfast in Findhorn, had a hot bath to warm up from the cold summer rain and headed out to the local pub for dinner.

I met a man who also owned a bed and breakfast and worked in Findhorn. The next day, I moved into his bed and breakfast. And he was even kind enough to show me around the Findhorn Foundation. I joined others in the meditation hall where I went into such a deep meditation that when I opened my eyes, all the other meditators had gone.

And there was a group of people having a staff meeting.

"Oh, sorry," I said. "I had no idea the meditation was even over."

They invited me to stay as long as I wanted, and were happy to see someone making the most of the wonderful energy there.

I wanted to have some body work done, because I was still aching from the nine weeks of two Bikram classes a day. I was guided to a lovely lady who did not do physical work, but worked on the energy body. She came highly recommended. After about two minutes of being quiet and laying her hands on me, she said, "What on earth

The Gift of Bikram Yoga

have you been doing? Your energy body is all over the place, and your chakras are all out of whack."

I told her about the gruesome nine-week yoga training and she said, "Whoa, that was intense. It'll probably take you about three months to integrate all that opening."

The next day, I found a brochure in the little shop for Callanish, the standing stones on the Isle of Lewis. And I knew, looking at the brochure, that I had to go there. The next morning after breakfast, I left for the West Coast of Scotland. The drive was beautiful. I kept shaking my head as to how beautiful Scotland was. The incredible range of colours of the mountains seemed so majestic that they could have been painted on. Every winding road displayed a postcard-worthy scene. I arrived at the ferry to get over to the Isle of Lewis late in the afternoon. I had no accommodation booked. My mum would really have freaked out.

I arrived on the Isle of Lewis at 9:30 p.m. and, as it was summer, it was still daylight. I walked around the streets, dragging my suitcase, knocking on bed and breakfasts until I found a vacancy. It took a while, but I found one just before 11:00 p.m.

The next morning, I caught the bus to Callanish. I had never heard of it before, but felt such a pull to go there. The morning was cold and rainy. As I arrived at the stones, a group of people were leaving, and I was the only person left. How lucky, I thought. There was a sign that said, 'No walking inside the stone circle'.

I looked around. Nobody was there. And I thought, I have to go in. It was not like me to break rules but the pull to go in was so strong.

I walked into the centre of the stones and felt like time stood still. I was drawn to a huge stone, and stood in front of it, leaning against it. I closed my eyes and started to hear music, very faintly. I could see in my mind a group of people holding hands in a circle and dancing around the centre stone.

It was a joyful occasion. I felt like someone had passed there, and they were celebrating his journey on to the next world. There were no tears, only joy, and the feeling like this person was being honoured for completing his time here.

As I leaned against the stone, my heart started to pound, as if I was running or doing some strenuous exercise. I talked myself into being calm, but it was a little frightening. Something was going on with my heart chakra, and I could only imagine. But it felt like it was being opened. I walked around, feeling such a familiarity there, trying to put my finger on what it was. It reminded me of the feeling you get when you wake from a dream, as it gently starts to fade and you try desperately to remember it. As the last traces of it leave your mind you are only left with a feeling; in the end no memory of the dream remains and the feeling has no reason for existing within you. I took many photos of the ancient stones, said to be older than Stonehenge. I felt very blessed to have this experience alone, even though I felt many beings around me.

I started walking down to the information centre. There was a group of people there and another one started coming up to the stones. There were soon people everywhere. How bizarre, I thought, that no one was there when I was around.

The rest of my trip was amazing. I still took deep breaths of awe during the drive, especially during the West Coast. I stopped in at Plockton, my favourite town in Scotland, where my second cousin owns the pub. We had a lovely night together, him and his wife and I. And I learned all about the town.

Plockton is situated by the sea. The streets are cobbled, and the gardens are incredibly beautiful and colourful. A stream of warm water from the gulf flows there. And it's warm enough for palm trees to grow along the front, surrounded by the mountains. Not a scene you'd expect in Scotland.

My favourite part was the Highland cows that roamed the streets. Big, red, hairy beasts with horns, that feature on many Scottish paraphernalia. Unfortunately, I heard not long after that visit that the cows had started to get aggressive with the tourists (well, they are Scottish, after all) so they had been put in a nearby field.

After my little trip, I knew that it was time to move on. I had no idea where. I did not really want to go back to Australia. I knew I wanted to be somewhere warm. I visited Ibiza with another yogi buddy, and we helped set up a studio there. I applied for many positions, and finally got my dream job on Maui, Hawaii.

CHAPTER THREE

Warning From an Elder

"Mai pale ike aʻo aka Makua."
"Do not set aside the teaching of your elders."

I was pinching myself as to how amazing Maui was. I had been studying my dialogue and aching to see just how much I knew. After my first class, a student came up and said, "How long have you been teaching, Norma?"

"Oh, that was my very first class," I replied.

She nearly fell over; she thought I had probably been teaching for about 10 years. I was off to a good start.

Teaching was nothing like teacher training. I had no nerves whatsoever. My classes just got better as I studied and practised, and threw my whole being into Bikram yoga.

Living on Maui in Hawaii, I felt like the luckiest girl in the world. Life was pretty special in paradise. I was teaching yoga, a yoga that I loved to teach. My previous corporate life felt like a past life now.

During my time on Maui, I found out about a course by Papa Kepilino. Papa Kepilino, or Papa K, as he was called, was a Hawaiian elder. He had never actually left his home island before and this was the first time he had permission from the other elders to leave his island and come to the island of Maui. Papa K had a smile from ear to ear. He had white, fuzzy hair, no teeth at all. He was overweight, had diabetes, and was in a wheelchair. This man lit up the room with his bellowing laugh and sparkling eyes.

I was so excited to learn the massage technique of Lomi Lomi, but to be honest, Papa really didn't give us much information about the technique of Lomi Lomi but more about the energy that he used whilst he was doing it. Papa K was very much a spiritual man and used prayer before any massage. In fact, prayer was really the foundation of his teaching.

During one session, his wife was talking and he wheeled over to me in his wheelchair and said, "You're going to have to be very careful, otherwise you'll end up like me."

I had no idea what he was talking about but he then explained, "You do the same as me, you take other people's energy into your physical body."

He called me a name in Hawaiian but I'm not sure what it was.

"You are going to have to be careful," he said warmly.

"You could end up very sick, that's why I am in a wheelchair," he said as his eyes lowered to the ground and the light in them seemed to fade. "Gifts sometimes come at a cost."

Warning From an Elder

The next day I was thinking about what Papa had told me about taking in other people's pain and I remembered someone else said exactly the same thing but I had forgotten about it. It had been a few years before and I was studying Reiki in Melbourne. There were only two participants on the course, myself and another lady. The other lady, unfortunately, had been shot in the Port Arthur massacre. The Port Arthur massacre was, to date, the biggest massacre that had ever occurred in Australia. This lady had survived, thankfully, but had been terribly traumatised.

As I was working on this lady and came close to her solar plexus area the teacher started screaming at me, "Norma, what are you doing, what are you doing, stand back immediately."

I stood back, almost in a daze. I felt hot all over and teary, and she looked at me and said, "Do you understand what you're doing?"

Of course, I didn't know, I had no idea, I just felt emotional.

She said, "Norma, you're taking in her pain, you're taking in her emotion, you can't do that. Go and wash your hands."

I went to the bathroom; I washed my hands all the way up to my elbows as I had been shown and came back out. The teacher explained what I had done. She said that when I was touching around or above the solar plexus area, where we hold a lot of emotion, I had taken it into my body. She pretty much said to me, "Don't you do that again," and moved on with the class.

Later on, I was the person on the table and the other lady was healing me. Again, I got in trouble because the teacher told me that even when I was supposed to be receiving the healing, I was giving healing and I was taking in her pain. I was very disappointed at the end of the weekend when the teacher said to me, "Norma, you can't do Reiki, you're far too open. You'll get very sick if you do Reiki."

As I remembered this, I wondered if anyone else had given me a warning at other times in my life. I remembered years before the Reiki, I had been in a health retreat in Queensland and while having a massage, the practitioner said to me, "Norma, this is what it feels like to carry your own emotion."

As he threw a towel on my back, a folded towel, I felt the weight of it.

He said, "You see, you can cope with this, this is your stuff, this is your emotions, we're all able to cope with our own stuff."

Then he put another towel on top and said, "Now, this is your partner's."

Then he put another one on and said, "This is your mother's," and another one, "This is your friend's," and another, and another, and another, until I had a whole tower of towels piled upon my back.

"Can you feel what that's like?" he said.

It felt heavy, it felt overwhelming. "You see, Norma," he explained. "This is what you do. You take in other people's emotions and this is why it feels overwhelming."

This was now three warnings I had been given about the same thing. Of course, it was really only beginning to sink in after this one from Papa K. I had forgotten about the other ones but they were all telling me the same thing—that somehow, I was taking in other people's emotions physically to my own body.

Years later, I was to learn that there was a word for what I was or what I was doing, and it was empath. I found out that there are many different types of empaths: physical empaths, who take in emotions to their physical body; emotional empaths, who feel—and as it turned out, I was both. No wonder people felt good around me because their darkness, their emotion, their sadness, their fear, their anger, came into me.

People used to say that a lot and now I knew why.

"Gee, I always feel good around you, Norma. You make me feel so good. I feel so much better when I'm around you."

Well, now I knew why: it was because I was taking on their stuff and they were walking away lighter.

Another memorable experience I had with Papa was that one day, one of the other students was massaging me. She touched a lump on my leg which was a hematoma from a fall I had had 10 years prior. It was the size of a golf ball and I hated having it touched. It happened when I had been rollerblading through Sydney's Centennial Park after having a few Chardonnays. I could not find the brakes on the rollerblades and when a car was coming straight at me, I had the choice of running straight into it or hitting the concrete path with full force, which I did. My leg was so black and blue that I remember feeling it throb for months.

The student called Papa over and told him about my lump. He said nothing, did nothing, but sat there for about 10 minutes and wheeled away. Later that afternoon, he leaned over to me and said, "The lump on your leg will be gone by the morning."

Sure, I thought, and smiled, not believing a word. The next morning in the shower I noticed my leg was not cold as it usually was. I rubbed the soap down it and nearly stopped breathing … The lump in my leg was completely gone.

Hawaii really was a magical place; I was really happy there. My days were filled with teaching yoga, practising yoga, swimming in the ocean. The friend that I shared her house with was an underwater videographer and invited me out many times on the boat she worked on. I got to jump off the boat, snorkel, swim with turtles; it really was a special time in my life and the depression I had experienced was a distant, grey memory.

I really didn't want to leave Hawaii but I only had a visa for three months so I had no choice. I decided to try and find a teaching position in another part of the world but nothing was showing up for me. Meanwhile, back in Melbourne, my car hadn't sold. All my furniture was still in storage so the plan I came up with was to go back to Melbourne for a short period of time, teach a little bit, sell my car, and come running back to Hawaii as quickly as possible.

The day came to leave Hawaii; I was really sad. A friend took me to the airport and said goodbye and all I could do was think of how long it would be before I could come back. At the check-in, the attendant lady with a beautiful big smile said to me, "What are you going to miss most about Hawaii?"

I said, "The aloha."

"But look at you, my dear, look at that smile," she said to her colleague. "You're taking it with you."

On return to Melbourne, I was lucky enough to find a place to stay with my dear friend Jack, in St Kilda. It was a beautiful house and Jack was happy for me to stay until I could find my own apartment. My days were busy. I was teaching in two studios, practising every day, and I also started a little clinic doing massage and clinical hypnotherapy.

In one of the studios I was teaching at, I was able to manage the studio while the owner was away getting married. I just loved teaching in the studios and developed a nice friendship with the studio owner as well. I was quite happy being back in Melbourne for a while. I found a lovely little apartment in Richmond but I didn't want to spend the evenings alone anymore. A friend of mine suggested that I try online dating. I was quite horrified at the suggestion. She assured me that there were some lovely, honest and decent people on the website and that I should give it a try. I had a look through and thought she might be right so I decided to give it a shot.

I was quite nervous about the whole thing. I had never had a blind date and I really didn't like putting myself out there. In fact, I had never even asked out a man, I was kind of old-fashioned. Anyway, times were changing and I didn't want to go to pubs and bars to meet someone so I put up my profile and within a week there were 160 interested parties. I went on six coffee dates with very different men. One of them became my new boyfriend and a new chapter of my life began.

CHAPTER FOUR

The Pinnacle of Happiness

"The happier the moment, the shorter."
Piny the Elder

Within a year I was teaching at two studios, doing massage, hypnotherapy, and dating my new man. I decided it was time to open my own studio. I found a wonderful space on top of a gym in a really popular street in Melbourne and I was so excited to tell the studio owner, Cassie, that I had found my own space. I expected a really excited response from her. Instead, she was furious, saying that she wanted to open another studio in that area. And said that because she already had a studio that she would receive preference from Bikram. After much deliberation, I decided not to apply for my new dream studio, just to let it go and let her have her second studio. I expected she would have been relieved about that. But Cassie was already fearful about me even considering the idea of opening my own studio and she immediately sacked me. We had shared many coffees and lunches together, with stories of our lives overseas, our trials of love and passion for Bikram yoga. I trusted her … I was devastated.

I couldn't understand why she would not be supportive of me. I honestly thought she would be so happy for me and we could continue our friendship as fellow studio owners, supporting each other and spreading this life-changing yoga.

One morning, soon after, I sat in meditation and I asked for my guidance to show me why Cassie was so fearful of me having my own studio. I was taken back to a conversation we had had earlier.

"Norma, I'm really jealous of your classes," she exclaimed loudly one afternoon.

I admire someone who has the decency to be honest and really respected her for saying that.

"Don't be daft," I said. "Everybody loves your class."

"No," she said. "They much prefer yours. You're a much better teacher."

"Well," I said, "what I believe is you have to teach like yourself. Don't try and be like anyone else. Don't try and be like me. Just be like you. That's what people respect."

When I was shown that conversation, it made me realise that's why she didn't want me to have my own studio. She was fearful that the students would follow me.

It was a difficult time for me because I wasn't able to practise anymore. I missed practising so much, but I just threw myself into looking for a new space.

"Don't worry about it," my boyfriend, Harry, said. "You'll find somewhere even better."

There were many sad weeks. But I KNEW I was supposed to be teaching this yoga and knew my new studio would already be there. I just had to find it.

It wasn't long before I found the most incredible space in Fitzroy. I had done some research and found out that Fitzroy had the highest amount of people per capita in Australia, so it was a great place to open a new studio. I was so excited when I walked around the building. I actually saw the students there already. I KNEW this was my new studio manifesting.

Cassie had other ideas. She had contacted Bikram and asked him to not approve my application to open my studio. I was dumbfounded because there were only three Bikram yoga studios in Melbourne. (There are now over 50.) I was going to forget about it and call it some other style of yoga, such as hot yoga, but then the fire inside me welled up and I decided to fight back at this insecure ex-friend who seemed to want to control my destiny.

I wrote to Bikram and explained to him about the demographics of Melbourne. There were no Bikram studios covering the north of Melbourne and between Fitzroy and the other studio there was a very busy road called Hoddle Street. Hoddle Street—every Melbournian's nightmare. I was sure students were not going to battle the traffic on this road every day just to do a class with me. I also explained to him how passionate I was about teaching Bikram yoga.

Within 48 hours I got a reply from Bikram, saying he had changed his mind and that I was approved to open my studio in Fitzroy. YES! I thought. Norma Strang, I said to myself, remember to ALWAYS fight back!

Financially, I had no idea how I was going to do it. I just knew that I wanted this more than anything and I was going to make it happen. The new studio space was fantastic. It was huge, two storeys. There seemed to be an enfolding vision in my mind of how I wanted it to look. I saw a podium. No other studio had one but I saw myself and other teachers teaching from that podium. I saw incredible carved furniture and a Buddha on the entrance hall. All of them came to life in my beautiful studio. My mind created and they manifested.

There was so much work to be done and so many challenges to overcome. Trying to get the Development Application from the council was one of the biggest challenges. They wanted an elevator put in for wheelchair access at an extra cost of $30,000 (obviously they had no idea how challenging Bikram yoga was!). I found out with horror the day before our opening day that there was no gas connected to the building. We had a gas heater connected, how could this be possible? This realisation came when we ran our first practice class the day before opening. The professional photography was done, advertising was running on schedule, flyers, mail drops all done, the website was up and running, advertising our big opening date. And after many stressful phone calls to the gas companies, I got confirmation that it would take a month to connect. Every time things seemed to be running along smoothly, there was another challenge. All were overcome.

Bikram Yoga Fitzroy opened a day before my 40th birthday on November 26, 2005. It was a success from the opening day. It looked amazing. The stunning wooden carved furniture came from Java. The reception displayed a fountain, Buddhas, incense, statues; it looked so beautiful. One day I was driving to work and I heard someone on the radio talking about my studio: "Have you seen the new yoga studio in Johnson Street?"

And the other presenter replied, "Yes, I've seen it. It's got a glass window and you can see in."

The Pinnacle of Happiness

At one point I was going to get blinds for the window but when the radio announcer said, "Yes, it's amazing. It's like a moving billboard!" I decided to leave the window without blinds for a while.

Harry had a drug and alcohol rehabilitation centre. I also was working there helping the residents, giving them massage and clinical hypnotherapy. I was teaching classes every day and practising every day, as well as running the 12 teachers that were also teaching for me. It was really busy and I loved it. One day, after attempting to do the advanced Bikram yoga, which I really should never have done, I dislocated my right knee. The pain was like nothing I'd ever felt before. I was screaming my head off. This new injury was to slow my life down completely.

I couldn't drive. I was on crutches. I couldn't teach for a while and I certainly couldn't practise. When I was well enough to get into the studio, I started to teach with my leg on a chair. Then I started to practise, but I was able to do very few of the postures. This was to become my dodgy knee. It never healed completely.

Two years into my relationship with Harry, he was sitting at the computer one day and called me over. He said, "Hey, which of these rings do you like?" He was on the Tiffany's website.

"Don't get me a ring, babe," I said. "Anyway, you'd never pick one that I would like."

"Sure I would," he said. "Come over and have a look." We scrolled through the website and there were three rings he had picked.

"Which one of those do you like?"

"That one," I said as I pointed to one.

The next day he took me to Tiffany's to have a look at it. I tried it on and it was just perfect.

"Of course you know," he said, "it will take me about five years to pay for that."

"That's okay," I said. "I don't mind waiting."

I'd never really wanted to get married. So wearing a ring was enough of a commitment for me. A few weeks later I was fumbling around with my crutches, getting ready to go out for dinner. Harry was standing at the doorway of my dressing room and he looked very nervous.

"What are you doing?" I said. He was fumbling around with a little box in his hand.

"Oh, it's not the way I wanted it," he said. "But I just can't wait. I want to give it to you now anyway."

"What is that?" I said.

And he opened the box to the most beautiful diamond ring.

"Will you marry me? I want to spend the rest of my life with you," he said as he teared up.

I literally stumbled back and fell off my crutch.

Mouth agape, I couldn't answer.

"Well, will you?" he said.

What is it that happens to women when they see a diamond ring? What does it really represent? Eternal happiness and joy. All the fairy tale stories rolled into that diamond ring. And I found myself saying, "Yes."

And then I laughed out loud and said, "Is this the most romantic place you could have proposed to me. In my wardrobe?"

Then we both laughed. He said, "I know we're going to our favourite restaurant tonight, but I just couldn't wait. It was burning a hole in my pocket. I had to give it to you."

From that moment on, I turned into a bridezilla. For someone that never wanted to get married, I was arranging everything in my mind. I wanted a beach wedding. I wanted to get married in a bikini. I just wanted maybe the two of us with some friends. It had to be very intimate and small and tropical. Of course, Harry had different plans. He'd never been to Scotland and said, "Why don't we get married in Scotland?"

"Scotland?" I said. "Are you nuts? It's cold. It's expensive. I want to wear a bikini." I laughed.

"Well, I thought it would be good for you to have your family there," he said.

He did have a way of always getting his way and he slowly talked me around to a wedding in Scotland. Next thing I was organising tartan fridge magnets, tartan candles, tartan wedding cake. If I could have found a tartan wedding dress that was nice I would have had that too. The wedding was getting planned very nicely and we started to discuss where it was we really wanted to live. I wanted to live in Hawaii, but that wasn't possible because Harry had his business in Melbourne.

"Can't we compromise?" he said. "Can't we find somewhere in Australia that's similar to Hawaii?"

So I started to have a look on the internet one afternoon. I decided to google Bikram yoga, and there was an article that had been written by a Bikram yoga fan.

She wrote, "Why is there no Bikram yoga in in Byron Bay? If Byron Bay is the yoga capital of the world and for me Bikram yoga is the best in the world, shouldn't there be Bikram yoga in Byron Bay?"

"Hey, Harry," I shouted. "What do you think of Byron Bay?"

I had been there years before just for a visit and I really liked it. The next thing we knew, we were looking at real estate in Byron. The first house we found got us so excited we were on a plane headed to Byron Bay. And before we knew it, we had bought it.

We got married in a castle in Scotland. It really was a fairy tale wedding and to think, I didn't really want this, and I had ended up loving every minute of it. My dress was like something out of *Gone with the Wind*. Spectacular Thai silk mother of pearl embedded with crystals, with flows of silk spreading down the aisle as I walked. We had an owl as the ring bearer that flew into the chapel and delivered our rings in a silk pouch.

As the moment arrived for me to be escorted with bagpipes into the chapel, the Piper asked me in his thick Scottish accent, "My lady, are you ready to meet your husband?"

"Absolutely," I said.

And I was. I walked down the aisle on my brother's arm. I was as nervous as a schoolgirl, more so because of my injured knee, wondering if I would trip, but there he was, my husband-to-be, looking so handsome in his kilt and a tear in his eye as he saw me. I was glowing with pride at meeting my prince to share our vows and our life together. I remember feeling complete when I signed the marriage certificate, as if my life was just beginning and everything up to this moment was gone. The wedding was a hit. All my Scottish friends from school, all the members of my family were there to celebrate that Norma was finally going to settle down. I never got to spend special moments with my friends and family, living so far away in Australia, so this was even more special to have all my loved ones with me.

The food was Scottish and well received and even my Scottish friends said it was the most Scottish wedding they had ever been to. The music was a mix of Scottish and disco and only the English relatives of my new husband sat out looking a bit sour-faced. The Scots did know how to party, and party they did. The dance floor was pumping from the start in a traditional Scottish way; we finished with Runrig's version of 'Loch Lomond'. The crowd circled around us as they sang their heads off and ran into the middle of the circle where my new husband and I stood in the centre. It was electric. The band was great. The chocolate wedding cake was the best anyone had tasted. Everybody was happy and had a great time.

After a honeymoon in the Lake District—I actually wanted the Maldives, but Harry got his way again—we came back to our new home, a six-bedroom house on 40 acres of beautiful green land, and a lot of overgrown land, a lagoon, a swimming pool, a three-car garage big enough to set up my new yoga studio. The day we moved in we ran around the house like children, shouting, "Honey, can you believe this is ours?"

It needed a lot of work, but we had time. I had sold my studio in Melbourne and done very well financially.

I used a large chunk of the money for a deposit on the house. We ripped out the carpet, polished the floors, painted the rooms, got a gardener, made the place look a million dollars, which it was now worth, well over, due to all the renovations. We renovated the garage and transformed it into the most beautiful yoga studio with male and female showers. We created a car park next to the lagoon and put in a new septic tank. It just looked amazing.

I seemed to create the vision and Harry had the grounding to make it happen. I was so happy. I told a friend that getting married was the best thing I'd ever done. Harry was my rock. He was my best friend. I felt so loved by him and had even learned to trust him, which did not come easy for me as he had a colourful past and I had had a lot of previous heartache. I loved him wholeheartedly. I thought we were invincible. One thing I did miss was passion, but I just thought that maybe this is what happened when you got married. I had always had passionate lovemaking in my past, but I was so content with everything else in my life that I succumbed to thinking that, well, nothing is 100% perfect. And it was a sacrifice I was okay with, but as time went on, that became a gap that I was missing a lot. Harry said he just didn't feel the urge and was content with the way that things were.

I tried seducing him dancing naked, all the usual things, but he was becoming more interested in TV—not a good feeling for a woman. I dreamed about passionate sex and that had a deep connection, but I still pushed it aside and got on with my till death do us part. I justified that it was a small sacrifice to be with a man I could finally trust. That was really the most important thing to me. My new yoga school was nearly ready. We had employed a town planner to discuss getting a Development Application, but he suggested that it was all too hard to do upfront and it was better to do it once everything was complete. As long as we did everything according to the guidelines, we would be okay. My new yoga school was a huge success. People came from everywhere and I only had two classes a day. I employed one teacher. And we got to jump in the pool after a hot, sweaty class and money was rolling in as I had hardly any overheads. Life was pretty darn perfect.

To make it even more perfect, in September of 2007, we brought into our lives the most treasured little being I had ever met. Hamish, the golden retriever. Hamish was the most adorable puppy. He became my shadow, following me everywhere. The only time we were apart was when I was teaching and as soon as I had finished, he would be allowed to come out and run around the yoga students. As happy as Larry, he was my angel in fur and I was totally in love with him. Harry had to go to Melbourne for work quite a bit and Hamish kept me company in the big house.

We had neighbours on the next farm over. They one time had owned all of the land, but had sold it some years back. We met them when we moved in. I told them I was going to open a yoga school and I invited their daughter who visited on the weekends to come anytime for free. The daughter was concerned about her father and asked us to keep an eye on him. She gave us her number for emergencies. The father was prone to wandering, having Alzheimer's. We were happy to help in any way. One day, one of my students found him on the bridge to our property, and on the shared road he had fallen and was bleeding. We called the ambulance who came to help. I left a message on the mother's phone to ask if he was okay afterwards, but there was no response, no thank you; I found this a bit strange. Perhaps she was embarrassed. On our first Christmas there I dropped in some chocolates and flowers and a card. I never went inside their house, nor did they visit ours, but we were very happy in our little bubble.

CHAPTER FIVE

The Bubble Bursts

"It's so much darker when a light goes out than it would have been if it had never shone."

John Steinbeck

After running the studio for only a few months, we received a letter from the council saying there had been a complaint about our yoga school not having a Development Application. I was concerned about the complaint and called my neighbour to see if it was her. I said, "Is there anything upsetting you about us running the yoga classes here?" She said, "No, not at all, and if I have anything to say, I'm the kind of woman who will face people." I said, "Oh, what a relief. I'm so glad you're not upset." I wondered who it could have been and she said, "Perhaps it was one of the other neighbours." I didn't know any of the other neighbours well. I had called the opposite farm a couple of times to ask them to remove their cows who sometimes got into our property.

The council said that the bridges on our road on to the property were old and could not stand many cars driving over them, so we got a quote to put in two steel bridges at $120,000. Even though we shared the road with our neighbours, we were prepared to foot the bill. We thought that would be it, but the council said that there were other complaints now and we would have to close down.

We were visited by someone from the council, who when he saw all the work we had done and how well it was set up, seemed genuinely sorry to tell us that we would have to close. He let it slip, I think intentionally, that it was our neighbours who had complained. I was gutted and furious at the same time. The day after the news, I passed the mother on the driveway and all the rage of a Scottish woman done wrong boiled up inside me. I rolled down my window and screamed at her, "It was you who made the complaint, you fucking two-faced cunt! And you had the cheek to say that you're a woman who faces people. I have students that are sick and need this yoga, even one with cancer. You're a fucking selfish old bitch." Her face went white, as she mumbled something about my language and not being very ladylike. I screamed, "Don't you fucking judge my language when you have the integrity of a Nazi."

I remember feeling deeply hurt beneath the anger and just wondered how people could lie like that. I never got that she couldn't have said she didn't like the cars driving on the road. There was not even a chance for us to open the other entrance to our property so that cars could have driven in that way. We did look into it, but it was too late and we were given a date to close the school. My students were devastated. Twenty of them wrote to the council and the mayor, pleading with them not to close. The letters just broke my heart. The student with cancer wrote to the mayor, "Please do what you can to save the school. I have cancer and since doing this yoga, the lumps in my breasts have diminished. I have reduced my chemotherapy and can play with my children again. Please do what you can to keep it open." My student received a cold letter from the mayor saying it was not her department.

I cried for days. I was angry for days. One morning I woke up so upset I rummaged through my drawer and found a flyer I had been given by a man for a meditation class. I needed something to help me feel at peace with all this. I went along and sat in the meditation room. The room felt clean and peaceful. There was soft music playing that seemed to soothe my heart. The facilitator started reading prayers from all around the world and I could feel my anger start to subside. I then felt two hands gently touch my shoulders. Tears started to fall down my cheeks and I was sobbing. The pain in my heart was so great: pain for the studio, pain for all my students, pain for me. The tears kept rolling down.

I heard the lady say, "If you need a tissue, put up your hand," and I gently opened my eyes. I could still feel the hands on my shoulders, but no one was actually standing behind me, as I had thought. She softly put a tissue in my hand and squeezed it with a comforting touch. I sobbed for the rest of the session. I told the lady what happened during the session and she said that there were spirit doctors working with us during the session. Those were the hands I felt. I left there feeling so much lighter. My anger was gone, my hurt somewhat diminished. I went there many times after that, but never felt those hands again.

My studio closed in November. Harry was keen for me to find a new place to teach and picked up my spirits by telling me the next one would be bigger and better. After months of trying to find a space that would suit our kind of requirements, we found a perfect place opposite the beach in Byron Bay. Harry had found it and dragged me excitingly to meet the landlord. I loved the place, but the minute I met the landlord, I instantly thought, I cannot work with this man.

He walked around the building like a puffed-up cockerel, boasting about how he owned this and that and how he knew how to handle the council. I tried to catch Harry's attention, widening my eyes at the landlord's ranting about how much he had done in the Shire and what he owned. But when I could get Harry alone, I said, "I don't like him. He has an ego the size of Australia."

Harry said, "It's a perfect location. Just smile and listen to the bullshit."

That was something I look back on as a moment in time where I should have listened to my intuition. This was the beginning of many lessons I was about to have. Listening to that knowing within, or in my case, not listening and getting such a kick up the backside for it.

Studio number three. The studio space was perfect. There was no cost spared. That's because I believed this would be the last studio I would ever open, so put everything into it. There were beautiful change rooms, the best tiles, four showers in the ladies', three in the men's. We sanded the floors, built the walls and the ceiling. Dave, the builder, who built my last studio, did an amazing job. He did ask me to get the landlord to stop interfering in his job and let him get on with his work, because the landlord had been popping in telling Dave what to do and Dave didn't like it at all.

I wrote an email to the landlord to do just that as carefully as I could, but he hit the roof. We needed a trip to the lawyers and a mediation to get through that one. At one point, Harry kicked me under the table and whispered, "Let him have his win." He was rambling on again about how important it was, but I did get a pat on the back afterwards for keeping my mouth shut and letting the landlord feel like King of the Jungle. Another time I did not respect my inner voice and truth. But we got through it and I learned to shut my mouth and let the landlord feel like he needed to, for now anyway.

We opened the following November. The classes were packed out from the start. Students from my Billinudgel studio and many more students came. It was pumping. The landlord had been a chore, but

The Bubble Bursts

true to his word, he did know how to handle the council and we got the Development Application. He even started taking classes after his wife had started and was looking and feeling great.

Harry received a call one day that made his face turn white. He wasn't shaken easily. He had such a colourful past. Having been a drug dealer and spent time in prison, I could not imagine what had him needing to sit down, but he had just found out that his key staff member had relapsed and stolen $50,000 from the business. That was the beginning of a challenging time. Harry had to spend a lot more time in Melbourne and I a lot more time alone. When he did return, he was so tired and stressed that he stopped doing yoga, and started to sit in front of the TV more and eat. He started to put on weight.

I asked him if there was anything wrong and he said to me, "If you ever leave me, that will be the end of me. I'll just move to an island and get back into drugs until I drop." I laughed and said, "Baby, that'll never happen. I love you. I'll never leave you. I'm just concerned that you're not happy." Harry had a way of keeping his mind busy if he was stressed. TV was one way and another way was shopping. He loved to shop, for me too. He had an incredibly generous heart but I was beginning to feel that shopping was a distraction and way of avoiding something emotional.

Then Harry decided that he wanted a dog too. He was strangely jealous of the love that Hamish had for me, but I was happy with Hamish and I didn't want another dog. But he talked me into it and said it would be better for Hamish when we travelled for him to have a companion.

Enter Brhide, or Brhide Baggins, as we called her, the naughtiest puppy ever. She was the opposite of Hamish: independent, stubborn and would not do anything she was told, but oh so adorable. Harry wasn't happy though because she bonded to me and not him. Well, I was feeding them, walking them, and spent every day with them, so I thought it normal. Hamish put up with the little ball of white fur, chewing his neck, biting his tail, stealing his toys, but a happy family nonetheless.

Harry decided that we needed to get away more and so we bought a Winnebago. I thought it was strange that when we did the paperwork, he put it only in his name, as the house was in both our names, but he said it would be better to put it in his business name. I was happy because I could take the dogs with me. Hamish found it hard to travel though. I bought him some travel sickness tablets and Rescue Remedy, but he really didn't like it.

One day, while practising yoga, I felt horribly sick. I vomited all over my mat and one of my teachers drove me home, having to stop the car for me to vomit again and again. I ended up in hospital with a cracking migraine, vomiting till there was nothing left to vomit. Harry stood behind me. "You're always sick," he said. "You need to eat meat. Do you know you've been in hospital seven times since we've been together?" He was right, seven times and many migraines, flus, colds, only to name a few. The next day I was standing in front of the bathroom mirror and I said out loud, "Why am I always sick? I eat well, do yoga, sleep well. What is it?" And my inner voice said, "It's because you take on all of Harry's stuff and the addicts he treats."

I stopped breathing because I knew it was true. I don't want to take on his shit, I thought. And then something happened. These words came out of my mouth as I looked in the mirror. "I now choose to end all contracts that I've made with Harry in this lifetime or any other lifetime, through all time, space and all dimensions, where it is not for the highest good, where I have agreed to take on his energy. In this moment, I send all his energy back to him and I am no longer responsible for him," or something like that. But it was very profound.

Within 24 hours, Harry had a back pain so bad that he had to take painkillers. He hated taking any form of drug, but he was doubled up in pain and had to take codeine. The next week he had a flu. In all our time together, he had not even sneezed, and now here he was, in bed with the flu so bad he had to cancel his trip to Melbourne. A week later, after returning from the Winnebago trip, I was rearranging my wardrobe and I came waltzing down the stairs in a Veronica Lodge gown, laughing and saying, "Hey, I found this in the …" And then I stopped.

I found Harry in his office on the computer with a terrified look on his face. "What are you doing?" I said with a sinking feeling in my gut. "Nothing," was the guilty answer. "Don't bullshit me. You're up to something." After a few minutes of this, he said, "I was watching porn."

"Why do you need to watch that when we never make love anymore?"

The next day I was sitting on the veranda and got a very strong feeling. I asked myself, "What's going on?" I had a strong feeling there was much more going on than porn watching. I heard my inner voice say, "Check the bedroom drawer." It was strange, I thought. I had just cleaned there a few weeks ago. What could I possibly find in there? But the voice was persistent. I went to the drawer, not to find anything strange, but to realise that an old packet of Viagra that had been in Harry's bedside belongings for five years was missing. My stomach churned. Harry had been to an AA meeting and came home all bouncy.

"Where's the Viagra?" I asked.

The look on his face told me something was very, very wrong.

"Oh, it's in the Winnebago," he said.

"Why would you put it there? We never use it." Okay, then. "Go and get it," I said in disbelief.

He froze. My stomach did a huge somersault and fear started sweeping through my body. After much fumbling around with words, he tried to find some composure.

"I took it to Melbourne, he said confidently. "I drove past a brothel but swear on the life of my son that I did not go in."

My stomach felt like it would fall through me as I remembered a quote I once read: "Lies are like cockroaches, for every one you see there are 14 or more hidden."

He left for Melbourne the next day, and I was left with the torture of lies, disbelief and confusion.

CHAPTER SIX

Betrayal

"You are going to break your promise. I understand. And I hold my hands over the ears of my heart, so that I will not hate you."

          Catherynne M. Valente

I asked Harry to come home when he was able to be honest with me. After all, that was something he taught.

"Get honest!" I would hear him yell at his clients on the phone.

Then he would remind me how all addicts lie. Sometimes I would forget he too was an addict, albeit in recovery.

I had hoped that he would jump on a plane and come home and tell me things were okay, but things were far from okay. I called him and asked him to see a therapist with me. I found a well-known therapist in Sydney who I knew would not let Harry outsmart him. Harry was himself a therapist and could fool the best of them.

I flew to Sydney and met him at the airport. It was like meeting a different man. He had changed so much; I could hardly recognise him. No loving embrace. No, "Darling, I miss you." No, "We'll get through this." Just coldness.

The previous week had been hell for me, just wondering what had gone on. Knowing something was not right, but he hadn't told me anything, so the gut-wrenching fear and anxiety was pumping through my veins for the whole week. I just wanted to know the truth.

We sat in the lounge, and I asked him if he was ready to talk. He took a packet out of his wallet and threw it on the table in front of us. It was a brand-new packet of Viagra. He had gone to the trouble of getting a new packet. But the packet that was in the drawer was five years old, old and tattered, and had even had some missing. I said, "Do you really think I'm that stupid, Harry?"

Then he sighed and poured out the truth. Well, maybe not all of it.

"I'm a sex addict," he said. "I've been going to prostitutes."

My heart nearly stopped, but at the same time there was a feeling of relief that I was hearing the truth.

"I'm a disgusting deviant, Norma. You would never begin to imagine the thoughts I have in my head."

I was in shock and finding it hard to walk out of the airport. When we did, a man wolf-whistled at me and Harry said, "Look, you won't find it hard to find someone else."

Betrayal

I was horrified. I didn't want anyone else!

We each had a session with the therapist together then on our own. It was so emotional for me. Harry never shed a tear. All he talked about was how he thought he could not give **IT** up. I stayed with a friend that night, and he stayed in a hotel. I wanted to meet up for dinner, but he said he wanted to go out and be free. I was inconsolable. I felt like my insides were being burned with acid, and the fear in every cell of my body was torture.

The next morning, we met. I knew he had been with someone else again the night before. He was acting so weird and sleazy. I felt like my Harry had been kidnapped and a sleazebag was in his place. However, at the therapist we both decided to try to make it work. I had to spend more time with him in Melbourne, and he had to be honest with me.

Back at the airport, we were chatting a bit. What would have happened if we had have split up? I said, "Well, you would have probably gone to Melbourne and left me in the house." He turned to me like the exorcist, leaned forward towards me, and said in a very scary, breathy voice, "If you take my house, I will fucking kill you."

My legs turned to jelly. My heart was thumping in my chest, and I was, for the first time in my life, terrified of my husband. I knew he meant it.

That night, getting home, he strutted around the house like a peacock. All I could do was think about how afraid I felt. I had put a lot of my money into this house, but he really did seem to think it was his house. I had a sleepless night, but knew that if I stayed in this marriage, I would become more fearful. Not just of him, but what he was getting up to. I felt that he had had a taste of something that he wanted more of, and I saw it destroying me. I had endured more than one previous relationship where I was lied to and betrayed and could not bear the thought of living in such anxiety again.

In the morning, I took him a cup of tea in bed and said, "I can't do this, Harry. I know you will act out more with this desire that you have, and it will kill me. I'd like you to leave." And that was it. We spoke to the therapist on the phone, and I told him I was afraid and not prepared to continue the relationship. The next thing, Harry was happily packing up his things in the Winnebago. He left the next morning, exactly three weeks after my chat in the mirror.

The day after he left, I was sitting on the veranda, and my inner voice said, "Go and check RSVP." "No way," I thought, having a conversation with this voice. "He won't even be in Melbourne yet." But I did check, and there he was. His profile name was Dr Harry, the same one that he had when I met him five years prior. He said on his profile that he was NOW ready to meet his soulmate or playmate. I was furious. He was still on the road to Melbourne. His profile picture was of him standing in front of the helicopter he had been having lessons with. Of course, to the reader, it looked like he owned it. I read his words: his favourite books, *Anastasia*, my collection, which he couldn't even understand. Oh, and bondage, obviously his. It was like he wanted to portray himself as a part of me and a part of him. I was so enraged that for a short time the heartbreak subsided. What I didn't know was whether that profile had been up during our marriage, or had he put it up in the last couple of hours? My guess was that it had been up during our marriage.

I came to that conclusion two years after our separation. I was having lunch with my sister-in-law Pam and friend Anna. Pam and I were discussing my wedding dress, which I had been trying to sell since the separation, when Anna said, "I have a friend who knows Harry; he paid for her to go through beauty school."

"Oh, that must have been after we separated," I said.

"I don't think so," Anna replied. "He told her that his wife owned the Bikram school in Byron Bay."

Betrayal

My stomach sank. Even after all this time it hurt like a blow to the stomach.

"How did she meet him?" I asked.

"She met him on the online dating service called SugarDaddy.com. She is a prostitute."

I could hardly breathe. Was I in denial all this time, thinking that my marriage had been so good and only went downhill a few months before the end? I was so confused and hurt, and felt like such an idiot.

The next few weeks were so hard. I was alone with no family. I couldn't eat. I was sick with grief. I took to drinking wine and smoking cigarettes, and on my 44th birthday he sent me two dozen white roses. I sat beside them and cried.

On Christmas Day, I reluctantly went to Pam's son's house for the usual family (Harry's family) Christmas dinner, but I could hardly eat. I looked skinny and sad, and all that kept me going was Hamish and Bhride. I left a couple of hours later, went home, and cried in my big, empty house. The next day, Pam told me that Harry had called his brother, so happy to announce that he had a new 34-year-old Thai girlfriend. My guess was, she was not so new.

That night, I went what might be called 'berserk'. I ran around the house, smashing all the love ornaments he had given me. I took a knife and slashed his leather chairs. I scraped the dining table. I got his kilt, the one he wore at our wedding, and I ripped it apart, and I sobbed myself to sleep. The next day, I got up and threw out what was left of the wine down the sink, soaked the cigarettes in water, put them in the bin and said, "Enough." It had been six weeks since he left.

We had the house on the market, so I had to keep it immaculate for inspections. I organised gardeners, cleaners, I did my share of keeping it perfect, but my heart was aching. One morning, I woke up to find the heads of my chickens ripped off. "A fox," the gardener told me. Then the new gardener put diesel inside the ride-on, and I had to get that fixed. I found out quickly that he liked to drink a lot, so I had to find a new gardener. One day, I heard squeaking underneath the cooker and found a litter of baby rats. Every little thing was overwhelming me. I cried as I put them outside under a tree, leaving them to nature.

Meanwhile, Harry was off to Shanghai to act out his addiction. Then Thailand. Then Shanghai again.

During this time, I had some help from a couple in the studio. Thank God for them. I had helped them with their teaching, and they were giving back support by teaching most of the classes. When I did go in to teach, I put on my teacher's face with a smile and collapsed in pain when I got home. The loneliness was agony. My mum would cry with me on the phone that she had gone through similar pain when my dad left her. She was reliving that pain listening to me. One day in the post, I received a necklace from my mum. It belonged to my nanny. It was a gold chain with a beautiful amethyst and tiny pearls tied around it. And the note from my mum said, "This was your nanny's. She was a strong woman. If you wear it, it may give you some of her strength." I put it on and cried and cried. I wanted so much for my mum to be there.

I had a trip to India booked, a pilgrimage to the Kumbh Mela with my Kriya yoga teacher. I had been initiated into Kriya many years before, but wanted to deepen my practice. I hesitated about going, but something told me that I had to get out of the house. One of my friends said, "Norma, how can you go to the Kumbh Mela with millions of people when you can't even go to Woolies in Byron Bay?" He was right. I could not stand crowds or gatherings of a lot of people. I was overwhelmed by their energy and felt bathed in their emotions. Nonetheless, I was going.

CHAPTER SEVEN

India

"Time spent in India has an extraordinary effect on one. It acts as a barrier that makes the rest of the world seem unreal."
— **Tahir Shah**

A healer in Byron had told me a few years earlier that I would go to India many times.

"Good Lord. India," I said. "I don't want to go to India. I'd prefer the Maldives."

How times and my tastes had changed. Not that I would not like to visit the Maldives, but at this stage in my life I was seeking something more spiritual, some answers to life, and a connection to something deeper.

The flight was long and my thoughts were filled with sadness about Harry. I wondered how long this grief would last. I was swamped with taxi drivers at the airport eager to get my fare on arrival. I had good instructions where to get a reliable one from the booking arrangements. As we drove through Delhi, I looked out the window at the filthy streets. The fog that fell all around was like pea soup, and all I could say to myself was, "Oh my God." My hotel room was freezing. Even sleeping in my clothes didn't make any difference.

The next morning, I got up super early to meet with a lovely girl I had met earlier at dinner the night before and we decided to go to the Taj Mahal together. I welcomed the company on such a long road trip. The drive was terrifying. The fog was so thick that we could hardly see in front of the car. There were so many accidents by the side of the road I wondered if we would arrive alive. We passed colourful trucks stacked with goods so high it was a wonder they did not topple over. Cows wandered the streets looking for food. Street dogs rummaged through the garbage looking like they'd never had much success. I was relieved to stop for breakfast. My travel companion and I ordered some breakfast in a large cafeteria. I was careful about what I ate but still would feel a little nauseous on the rest of the trip.

As cars are not allowed too near to the Taj Mahal because they produced too many fumes and could potentially stain the colour of it, we were transferred to a rickshaw, which took us into the grounds of one of the New Seven Wonders of the World. My first view of the magnificent building actually took my breath away. The arduous journey felt so worth it to witness the Taj Mahal. I had never seen any building quite so spectacular. The shimmering mother of pearl colour in the sunlight was so breathtaking I had tears rolling down my cheeks. What a strange response, I thought, to cry at a building. But oh, what a building. I quickly understood why it was one of the New Seven Wonders of the World. We learned the story of the great king who built it for his love, and I remember thinking, oh, to be loved with such depth.

India

The trip back seemed easier as we stopped at the birthplace of Krishna and bought some trinkets. Arriving back at the hotel, I was not even bothered about my cold room, but thankfully my request for a room change had been granted and I fell into a blissful sleep after my first memorable day in India.

The next day we headed for Haridwar, where we met the rest of the group on a bus trip that took seven and a half hours. I was so glad to get to Haridwar. Our hotel was called Hotel Chille. I was to share a room with my Kriya yoga teacher and friend, Rohini. It was humbling, to say the least. We even had to share a bed, so we put pillows in between us and made do with our little room. I was so excited to be in India.

The next morning, I woke up dizzy. The dizzy feeling stayed with me for some time. I was told that a lot of spiritual seekers experience strange sensations when they come to India. We had a camp set up in the grounds of the Kumbh Mela. We walked each day to our tent where we meditated, chanted and prayed. One morning, a group of Naga Babas came to meet our camp and our teacher. They had heard that he was teaching about the great Babaji and wanted to meet him. The Naga Babas were said to be one of the most spiritual and disciplined group of yogis, who rarely ventured down from the Himalayas, but the Kumbh Mela was one time they did. We were so excited to be in the presence of such sadhus (holy men). They had long dreadlocks tied on top of their heads. They wore orange robes for the occasion, even though we were told that most times they were naked and covered in ash. They invited us to their camp, which we could not wait for.

After a few days, I found myself most unimpressed with the group teacher. He was very aloof and hardly talked to the students. He sat with his wife at dinner and didn't speak to anyone. A few others felt the same. I shared my disappointment with Rohini, my teacher. She said she had mentioned that he was too aloof in the past to him, so she bluntly told him that I felt the same about him. She said, "You know, Norma is a teacher of Hatha yoga and has her own yoga centre.

She would be great as a Kriya yoga teacher, but she too thinks you are aloof and don't interact with your students."

I nearly fell off my seat laughing when she told me. I loved her honesty.

The people in the group made up for the teacher. Some I could talk to for hours. It was so refreshing talking with people who were on the same wavelength as me. I loved the chanting and the meditation.

One day, we all went to the River Ganges. As it was a sacred day, we were encouraged to take a dip in the incredibly fast-flowing Ganges. There were rails to hold onto so that we did not get washed away. No bikinis here. Ladies had to wear their long Indian Punjabis. When I went in, Rohini started singing, "ooooooom Ganga." Again, she had me in stitches as I held my nose with one hand and the rail with the other hand and slipped my whole body under the chilly water. It felt amazing. I had heard such stories about how dirty the Ganges was, filthy with dead body parts and rubbish. This was sparkling clean. My head felt strangely dizzy again when I came out. It felt exhilarating, but strange.

When I started to walk with the others back to our hotel, I realised I was limping. It was a few years since I had had surgery on my dodgy knee, but I had not limped for a long time. I was limping now, and the next day my leg was so sore I had to borrow a walking stick. Eventually, the pain was so bad that I could not walk to camp. I had to get a ride on the back of a motorbike.

I had heard so much about Rishikesh I was so excited to visit it. We travelled by bus along the bumpy roads. We visited the ashram of Sivananda, where we took pictures and meditated: a strange modern combination. We then went to the Kriya Yoga Ashram and met the Baba, who took us into a wonderful circular meditation room, which had beautiful statues of Babaji, Lahiri Mahasaya, Sri Yukteswar and Yogananda. The room was filled with orbs. The 12 astrology signs were all around the room. We got time to sit in meditation and view the rest of the ashram, which was being extended. Some of my group went on to stay at that ashram after the pilgrimage. I heard it was freezing cold and I was glad I had not joined them; even though I was Scottish I did not handle the cold very well.

The streets of Rishikesh were a feast for the senses. The smell of Indian food filled the air. Street sellers tried to sell us their goods as we passed by, some with no teeth but beautiful smiles. I stood and watched my very first snake charmer and I thought, well, I have known a few men who reminded me of him. With his flute, he charmed the cobra out of its box. The shops were filled with jewels of many colours, and according to the Ayurvedic astrologers, the right stone worn on the right finger could help one avoid disaster and draw good things to you.

My new friend Chris and I could talk for hours. We decided to go for lunch and ordered the same thing. Within an hour I was feeling quite ill, but Chris was fine, so it couldn't have been the food. My head was throbbing. We joined the rest of the group to witness a choir of orphans singing on the banks of the Ganges. I was so disappointed that I felt so bad. What an incredible gift to witness and I was in such discomfort I could not absorb the beautiful chanting. I was aching to get back to my little hotel room and my bed. When the teacher announced we were going to stay on the banks of the Ganges for evening sadhana, I nearly cried. I found a seat beside my friend Daniel.

"Are you okay?" he asked. "No," I said. "I feel awful and I'm beginning to feel sick, too."

The group started their sadhana with closed eyes, and I started to cry and cry and cry and cry. My headache was now a migraine. It was like all the pain from the past was welling up inside me and pouring out through my tears. Then I grabbed Daniel's arm.

"I'm going to throw up," I whispered.

He looked around and pointed to a wall.

"Throw up there," he said.

"I can't do that," I replied. "There's a beggar sitting there. Looks like life is bad enough without some tourist throwing up on him."

Then he pointed to the flowing river in front of us and said, "The Ganges!"

I turned and ran down to the Ganges and threw up in it. One day bathing in it, one day throwing up in it.

The trip home was agonising. I vomited in a bucket most of the way back. Daniel didn't leave my side and escorted me to my room when I vomited all over the bathroom floor. Over the next 24 hours I was visited by most of the group, offering everything from Advil to acupressure. I was so touched by this group of people that only a few days ago were complete strangers to me. The next morning, I woke up congested with a flu. Rohini brought me porridge and left to go to the group camp. She told me that some seekers get a spiritual cleansing in Rishikesh that can be like a purification. I slept and cried all day. Where on earth are all these tears coming from? I thought. I spent the next day doing the same. I also had developed a horrid skin rash since arriving in Haridwar, so I seriously was not looking my best.

The next day I was so happy to be feeling a little better so I could join the group in meditation at Shivananda's cave in the mountains. There were too many of us to go in deep to the cave at once, so we took turns. As I walked outside the area, there was a little monk chanting in Sanskrit. He sounded so beautiful. I passed him, respectfully bowing my head. Later, the group came out and went for a walk on the Ganges. I wanted to go inside the cave alone and meditate.

I felt so blessed when the little monk came in to meditate as well. I hoped he would chant. I was sitting with my sore leg outstretched. He surprised me by pointing at my leg, as I was not sitting correctly. I told him in sign language that my leg was sore. He came over and put his hand on my knee. Oh, I thought, he's going to give me a healing. As he asked me to stand up, I was ready for some miracle from the little monk, and then the unthinkable happened: he tried to kiss me and pushed his body against me, looking like he was going to cry. "Please," he begged. I pushed him off and ran out of the cave. I found Rohini and said, "Fuck! I've just been groped by a monk in a cave."

I laugh my head off now as I write this up, at how naive I was, but I was pretty upset and felt like a star goose at the time. What a lesson in not respecting anyone in an orange robe.

The only time the Kriya yoga teacher talked with me was after this. He was very annoyed and told the resident Baba. The poor monk was dragged in front of me and made to go on his knees and beg forgiveness. I was asked if I wanted police and I said, "No," and then he was thrown out of the ashram. I felt awful. "Please don't throw him out," I begged, but it was too late.

The charges for this were pretty bad; it could have been a lot worse for him. They explained he was not a resident of the ashram, he came to chant in the Sanskrit prayers. I found solace in the hope that this whole incident may have prevented him from doing anything worse to other women. As we left for our hotel, one of the group members, who resembled Jesus, said to me, "You really are doing a lot of spiritual work here, Norma, a lot of cleansing."

"Oh yes," I said. "I'm limping like a cripple, I've thrown up in the sacred Ganges, I have the worst flu of my entire life, my face resembles a pizza, and I've been groped by a chanting monk. Yes, I feel so spiritual." I laughed.

Undercover Angel

The rest of the pilgrimage was much lighter. My thoughts of Harry seemed to be easing. We visited the ashram of Lahiri Mahasaya. It felt so amazing to sit in this spot where he meditated, in his prayer room. We visited the ashram of Anandamayi Ma, where a didgeridoo player was playing, of all things. I loved it there. I smiled the whole way through my meditation. In the morning, I said goodbye to the group. I had a tear in my eye, I truly loved sharing my time with those people, and I headed off to New Delhi in a taxi with the wife of our teacher. It was a long, hard trip.

After the flight to Bangalore, I found my way to the ashram of a very well-known Swami. My friend had an apartment there and assured me what a wonderful experience I would have. I arrived still limping from whatever happened in the Ganges experience. I was brought immediately to an in-house shop where I was told I needed to buy my own sheets, Indian clothes and bindis for my third eye. It had already cost me $1,008 for the stay. Already I was suspicious. I was then taken to a desk amongst many desks where senior, more spiritual disciples, looking very unspiritual and stressed to me, were taking the details of new recruits. Apart from being mostly German people, the atmosphere made me think of Nazi Germany. Seriously. This was not what I had in mind for a meditation retreat.

After I gave all my details, including a photo of myself, I was shown to my room on the third floor. Oh boy, I thought, this is going to be interesting, as I limped up the steps, dragging my suitcase. Why couldn't I be like normal Scottish people and just drink too much on the weekend and forget my troubles? Nope, not me. I go searching for happiness in the weirdest of places.

I quickly learned that it was far from a relaxing place to meditate. The next morning, I woke up in tears. Why the hell am I here? I thought. Then there was orientation from a stressed-out Fräulein, which seemed to be the emotion of the entire group, who seemed to silently scream out for Valium or a good orgasm, the latter probably most in need.

There were rules galore.

- Shower each time before entering a temple, three times a day. That means three outfits a day to be laundered in the ashram, and paid for, too. Do not leave your room without a bindi on your head. Instant suspicion to what that could be about.

- Never enter a temple if you are menstruating, and wear a coloured band on your arm to show the whole fucking world that you're on your period. Never serve anyone food if you are on your period. God forbid, they may die.

I stayed back after the stressed-out Fräulein left and spoke with my friend. Bharati was also German; I adored her.

"What's with asking for all the money?" I said. "It's already cost $1,008 dollars to come here."

"Oh, it's because Swami is giving us so much," she replied.

"Like what?" I asked.

"He helps your spirit evolve and balances your karmas." What a crock, I thought. How can everyone not see through this guy? That night, I had my first sitting with Swami. I honestly had no idea what he was going on about, but the whole room of people seemed mesmerised by him. This 30-something dude in a brown velvet jacket who did not like to be stared at, to me, was an Indian version of Arthur Daley. What had I done?

The next morning I woke up with severe constipation, which I was told was because I was not accepting. I put it down to the mushy food with no fibre myself. A doctor came to my room and gave me some heavy-duty laxatives, which still took a few days to work. The next day, Swami met all the women and asked us what we wanted. Peace, happiness, love, purpose came to my mind. But no, we were supposed to want a connection with his lineage. Then he did a ritual; there were a lot of rituals. We had to draw a yantra 108 times to connect with his lineage.

The festival of Shivaratri actually was upon us. The whole ashram was getting ready for the most important night of the year, the celebration of Lord Shiva. The ashram pretty soon reminded me of a trip to Las Vegas back in my days working in the car industry, although Vegas and the company I was with then was much more fun than this. Neon lights were all over the place. It was really quite gnarly. So it finally arrived, Shivaratri, the night you can ask for whatever you want from Lord Shiva and it would be given to you. So I thought about it, I joined in, asking for my three things, one of them being to heal my knee. Everyone sat cross-legged in meditation, and I always had to find a cushion and stretch out my leg, almost always annoying the person in front of me. This night was the same.

I decided to go back to my room and use the toilet and escape the boring rituals. As I went to walk up the steps sideways, the only way I could without pain, I realised my knee was not hurting. I walked up and down the three flights of stairs without pain. When I got back to my spot on the floor, I sat down, and for the first time since my injury I crossed my legs. No pain, no need to stretch out. I was able to sit in meditation now. This little man in his brown velvet coat now had my attention.

The next day we were taken to a spot on the land where we were told about having a power spot. Swami said, "To reach enlightenment, we must have one."

Basically, we had to put our thumb in some earth from the fire ceremony ash and put it in the earth, bury it, meditate on it when we get home. I walked away before they had finished explaining the details when I found out how much it would cost. There was no way I was leaving my DNA in the grounds here, because that's exactly what was going on. Swami had other intentions, though, for me.

That night, we were all sitting with Swami, dressed in our whites, our bindis on, our malas around our necks. I had just shared with my roommate that I would not be doing this power spot thingy when Swami locked eyes on me. I mean, stared into my eyes. It felt like 15 minutes. As he did, I saw a vision in my mind of Jesus on the cross, me crying at the foot of the cross, and a loving hand reaching out to comfort me. It was the hand of Swami. I saw this. I said in my mind, "You were there too." He smiled and his eyes finally let go of mine. I have no idea what happened, I felt he was putting these images into my mind, but I changed from that moment on. Next morning, I was up, putting my thumb in the earth, creating my power spot.

I spoke to my friend about that and asked what could have possibly happened, and she said it was his intention. She said perhaps he had seen us chatting together and was suspicious that I was not fully a believer like everybody else. She thought that he had done something to me. I thought so too. Perhaps a holographic insert. I found out years later what a bad decision this had been. I don't know how long it took me before I realised this man was taking my energy, but I remember throwing out all his photos, books, yantras and anything from the ashram. But how much damage had been done after the hours of yantras I had done, three hours of chanting under the full moon, smashing coconuts, and goodness knows what else, all in the name of searching for some inner peace?

CHAPTER EIGHT

Visit From a Friend

"A friend is one that knows you as you are, understands where you have been, accepts what you have become, and still, gently allows you to grow."
— **William Shakespeare**

I arrived home, walked into my house and thought, I don't want to live here anymore. I felt like a stranger in my once dream home. It was empty, filled with sadness and echoes of the sound of crying. Within a week, I had moved into a little house in a nearby suburb which felt a lot like an apartment after my six-bedroom, 40-acre home. The move had taken a lot out of me.

Harry was back and forth to Shanghai. Meanwhile, I was left to pack up the house alone. My new little rental house was sweet, but I was eaten alive by mosquitoes every time I went outside. Hamish had blood on his nose from bites. I couldn't even sit outside, they were so ferocious. Now I knew why the landlady left bottles of mosquito spray in the kitchen.

I seemed to be still in shock about the whole thing. When I wasn't teaching, I was at home listening to Eckhart Tolle, trying to get out of the sadness of my mind. Actually, his voice helped me sleep; that was always better than being with the thoughts in my mind. My days consisted of going to the studio and appearing that all was okay, when inside, I felt like I was dying. I had no problem putting on a show on the podium and cracking the whip to encourage the students to find their strength within.

If anything, my situation encouraged me to encourage my students more to find that strength.

"Come on," I would say. "How are you going to cope if you lose your lover or your business or your home or your position or your health or someone you love dies? You have to be strong, in case if any of those things happen to you."

Little did I know in the coming years, I would endure every single one of those losses.

For some reason, when I was teaching, all my pain went away. I was present in each moment with whatever was going on in the room. I had the ability to read people, and if they were struggling or being lazy, I would say, "Hey, Michelle, are you sitting down because you're struggling or because you're being slack?"

I would get a refreshing honest answer back: "Because I'm being slack," she would reply with a smile.

I loved that kind of honesty. I would laugh and say, "Thank you for being so honest. Then whenever you're ready, join us."

Visit From a Friend

Most of the students loved my class. Some avoided them, usually the lazy ones, but I had no joy in teaching lazy people anyway. The most challenging students for me to teach came from other studios, where they were taught with a lot less discipline. Sometimes my students would travel and come back and tell me stories of visiting other studios.

"Oh, you come from Byron?" the teacher would ask. "Then you can go straight to the front row. Norma's tough."

This usually came from someone who had never met me or taken my class, but had heard the stories of how tough I was. If they only knew what I was trying to teach my students with this toughness. I often heard the students laughing after class.

"Did you hear how she handled that, the rude guy? It was brilliant."

I had no problem telling people they were being an asshole or a drama queen or an attention seeker. In fact, I seemed to be able to say exactly what other people were thinking, but were too afraid to say.

I knew when someone was going to be sick or drop before it happened. One day a student at the back caught my attention. "She's going to faint," my inner voice said. I jumped off the podium, but before I could get to her, one of my students was heading for her. I called her name and told her to kneel down and keep her eyes on me. The student said, "My guides said I need to help her."

This was quite common in Byron Bay—the mention of spirit guides. I said, "Well, just go back to your mat and tell your guides that I'm the teacher and I've got this."

Snickers came from the rest of the class as I took care of the student who informed me she had not eaten and was dizzy. A coconut water was given to her to replenish her sugars, and a lie-down, and she was able to finish her class.

In between teaching, I was making sure the house was neat and tidy for inspections. Harry was usually overseas, so I was left with the burden of driving up to the house, which I really began to detest, organising the gardeners and the cleaners and heading back to my little rented house with the dogs. I often thought, if I didn't have my dogs, would I have the desire to continue on? I loved my dogs so much. I could not bear to think of them getting separated or put into a shelter. No, that would never happen to my babies, I would soldier on.

One day I got a letter from a lawyer saying I was getting sued by a yoga studio nearby.

Fuck, what now? I thought.

A girl had written to me a month or so back and asked me to mentor her, as she had heard that I mentored teachers. I had told her that I could only mentor her if she was trained in Bikram yoga, not the yoga that was being offered at her studio. I urged her to do some research before she did her training and explained that if she wanted to teach Bikram at a Bikram Yoga Centre, she'd have to be trained by Bikram.

I was being sued for slander, because I tried to help the girl. Turned out, the studio was trying to sue another Bikram school too, because he had told the girl the same. I just did not need any more stress. At that moment, I fell to my knees in tears. Later that day I had to speak to Harry about the house, and again, I burst into tears.

"You're in overwhelm," he said. "You know you've been through two of the most stressful situations in the last few weeks: you've separated and moved home. These are major causes of stress."

"I'm not coping," I said. "I'm exhausted and I'm stressing about next month's rent; things are slow at the studio."

"I'll lend you the money," he said. "We can fix it up in the settlement. Don't worry, I will take care of you."

What did that mean, he would take care of me? Was that because we were still married and he felt obliged? I cried all night.

Sure enough, the money came through the next day. In the description box he had written, "From Harry, who still loves you."

My heart was breaking in pieces, I was so confused. A few days later, he called me and said that he felt he had made the biggest mistake of his life and felt like committing suicide. I urged him to come and talk and see me, but he never did.

My friend Bharati came to stay to run a meditation course in Byron. She told me she only ate raw food. I had done two courses on raw food, so I decided to make some of the dishes. Bharati had eaten raw for 16 years; she looked 15 years younger than her age. Her skin was flawless and she radiated health. She also meditated up to eight hours a day at times. She told me to watch a movie called *Simply Raw* which was about a group of people who had diabetes.

They gathered together in the home of a raw food teacher called Dr Gabriel Cousens. I loved this movie and seeing their health could be improved by eating raw food. This was the introduction to my new passion. I bought every book I could find on raw food, went into the kitchen and that became my place of healing.

Before I switched my body over to eating raw, I did an eight-day colonic cleanse, which I had done twice a year for the past few years. This time I ate raw food; normally I didn't eat at all. I cannot believe that by eating raw food, I lost more weight than eating nothing. I felt amazing. As soon as I got home from teaching or practising at the studio, I'd be in the kitchen experimenting. I was pretty surprised with most dishes, inviting friends who were equally surprised at how tasty the food was. Some dishes ended up in the bin, but I would try again until I had perfected it. I soon noticed that not only was my body changing into a much leaner version, but I was feeling happy again. Who knew that food could make you feel so good?

The only thing that was stressful at this time was my studio landlord; he was beginning to bully me. For no reason at all he would call and say, "You need to do this or you haven't done that," then he would shout and swear at me for something. I realised that he never spoke to me like this when Harry was around. He was also coming to my classes, but never behaved like this when he was there.

One day, both he and his wife were in class. I noticed that she was freezing and staring off into space. It was so strange, because she had developed a beautiful practice and was looking so well and happy. She had been coming to a class for a few weeks, but he had just started. I caught her after class and said, "Hey, what happened to you in there?"

She said, "I can't do it when he's in the class."

I knew what was happening; I could not tell her. He was taking her power. He did not like that she was looking and feeling so well and was developing a new confidence.

Narcissists can't stand when their partner outshines them. So that's why he started to come to class. "Come at a different time," I suggested. "He wouldn't let me," she said. My heart went out to her.

One day my landlord was in class; his wife was not. I asked to talk to him, as he'd sent me a threatening email saying I was late with rent; I was not. All the payments were up to date, proving I was not late at all, but this is what he liked to do. After class I called him over and said, "Tom, did you get my email showing all the receipts for the payments and I am up to date?"

Visit From a Friend

"Yes," he said. "You don't owe us anything, it's all up to date."

Of course, there was no apology for this horrid accusation. He said, "You must get the air conditioner serviced." Moving on to another subject and order.

"I'll get a quote," I said.

"I can get my guy to do a quote too," he said nicely.

This was another thing he did, nice then nasty. I sometimes wondered if he was bipolar.

"Well, that would be great," I said.

That evening I got a call from him, swearing and screaming at me that if I did not get the air conditioner serviced, I was in breach of the lease. I could not believe it after he'd said he was going to get a quote. I tried to remind him of that, but he was just going off.

I came to the conclusion that he perhaps had had a fight with his wife and was letting off steam by dumping on me. Maybe I was imagining it, but I had had enough. I dropped my head on the desk and cried. I would never put up with a student treating me this way. I would tell him I would no longer teach him.

I slept on it overnight, just to make sure I wasn't reacting from the emotion, but the next day I felt the same. It was still clear that I no longer wanted to teach him or have him bully me. I wrote the email telling him that I did not want to teach him and to find another yoga teacher, to just be my landlord.

The next day, I received a letter from the landlord's lawyer saying that if I did not pay the money I owed him within 24 hours, he would be taking legal action. Of course I didn't owe him any money, but he could not stand someone, especially a woman, standing up to him. But it wasn't the first time. A pregnant girl who worked at the reception at the back of the resort had taken out an AVO against him. I contacted my lawyer and spent the next year and thousands of dollars proving that I did not owe him any money.

During this time, Tom switched his lawyers more than once. My lawyer said he would never work with someone like him, and no wonder, his lawyers are probably coming to the same conclusion. In the end, he just withdrew the claim. My lawyer said, "He just wanted to punish you, Norma, for standing up to him."

One night I had a call from Melbourne, from my friend Laura. She was a hoot. She made me laugh and always had a heart of gold. She had worked with me in the car industry, sat with me in a Melbourne cafe when I told her of my dream to leave the advertising position I was in at the *Herald Sun* and find more purpose to my life.

"Go for it, doll," she said. "Most folks only dream of doing these things."

Tonight she was calling me to say, "Norms, I've just seen a movie called *Eat Pray Love*; it was bloody fantastic. It reminded me of you so much, with all your meditating in India and living in Spain. Well, I thought this is bloody Norma, except your life is much more tragic. You should write a book, honey. It would be a bloody bestseller."

I laughed my head off and said, "Please come and visit."

She had been to visit the year before for my birthday. I missed her so much. I was over the moon when she said she would come again. Laura liked to drink, but she knew that her time with me would be a healthy one with so much to catch up on. The last time I'd seen her, I was happily married in my home with my yoga studio in Billinudgel, my favourite studio, and she was working in a job she loved. She had recently lost that job and was pretty cut up about it.

Visit From a Friend

I talked about my heartbreak and my newfound passion in raw food. She opened the fridge and said, "Everything's bloody green, Norma. That's just wrong.com."

She had me in stitches and also shared how she was devastated at the loss of her previous job. She felt betrayed and used by her boss after she was let go, and she was in the process of trying to get quite a bit of money that he owed her. I felt so angry, because I knew how Laura worked so hard. Of course, I did not know her employer's side of the story, but Laura was my friend and I could feel her heart.

We did yoga, prepared healthy meals, and on Sunday, I took her to the colourful Bangalow markets. I loved the markets in the Byron Shire. Harry and I went most weekends. I had not been for a while, so it was lovely to go again. I took her to have a tarot card reading with a lovely lady called Rita, who had read for me a few times. Laura had her reading, whilst I sat in a drumming circle with my chai tea, watching the colourful scene of people dancing and smiling.

When I went to have my reading, Rita said to me with concern, "Norma, you must help Laura."

"What do you mean?" I said.

"She needs help," Rita said.

"She won't tell me the deep stuff, Rita," I said. "She avoids deep and meaningfuls."

"She feels shame," Rita said. "Try and get her to talk."

So in the car on the way home, I told her what Rita had said.

"You need to talk to me, Laura. Please tell me how you're feeling."

After a long pause, tears started to roll down Laura's face.

"I hate myself, Norma. I'm a bad mother."

"What rubbish!" I said. "Laura, you're wonderful and I've seen you with your kids, you're indeed not a bad mother. Where does this shit come from?"

"I just never feel good enough," she said. "And losing my job makes me feel it more."

My heart was breaking for her. Over the next few days, she shared some more of her pain. I encouraged her to keep up the yoga, to stop drinking. She was feeling better after a few days with me, so I urged her to continue the path. A few weeks later, she called me and was so excited to tell me she had another job and was doing Bikram yoga. I was so pleased to hear her happy again.

It was getting close to a year since I separated. I had spent that time licking my wounds, never thought about dating, as some friends had suggested. I really could not imagine being with another man. One day I received an email from a man from the studio saying that he was not feeling great like everybody else after class and wondered if he was doing something wrong. I tuned into him and felt he was going through a lot of emotion. I wrote him an email explaining a bit about yoga and the emotions and how I felt he was perhaps being too hard on himself and to keep going.

He wrote back and thanked me, saying he would indeed keep trying and asked if I was psychic. I responded by saying that it's easy to feel pain in others, when you have experienced pain too. Over the next few weeks something strange started to happen. I had seen that man in the studio just a few brief minutes since his email. Once he was at the reception, he seemed a bit nervous and uncomfortable. Once in my class, I started to have dreams about him every night. I have heard that when these kind of dreams happen you could be about to meet someone with a karmic bond to you. (That does not always mean good things.)

When I saw him at the studio the next time, he took my class and asked me afterwards where I walked the dogs and said he would look out for me on the beach. How weird, I thought. I didn't find him attractive at all, I wonder why I was dreaming about him? But the dreams continued. One night I gathered the students after class. Things were getting a bit slow at the studio and my energy levels were just not what they used to be. I decided to cut down some of the classes.

The man was in the class that night too; he had only taken two of my classes. As I shared with the students about the schedule change, I could feel the disappointment, but at this stage, I had no other option.

The next day I received an email from the man in my dreams. He said he would like to offer his help, as I had been kind to him at a tough time in his life by showing him kindness in my email at a time when everybody else in his life was less than kind. He said he helped businesses and perhaps he could give me some ideas to help mine, so I agreed to meet him for a coffee.

CHAPTER NINE

New Boyfriend

It's not that I'm afraid of falling in love, I'm afraid of falling in love with the wrong person . . . again."
— *Ana Chable*

I met Charles at a local beachside cafe I went to regularly. He was waiting for me when I arrived. He stood up to greet me nervously and announced that he'd brought champagne. How strange, I thought, it's 10:00 a.m. in the morning. I smiled and said that I did not drink alcohol at that time of the day and would stick to coffee. He said it was his anniversary, he'd been in Australia for one year to the day. He was born in Australia but had moved to Europe and lived there for over 25 years. We ordered breakfast, and got talking. Not much about my business as was the plan, mostly about him. I sensed he was a drinker by the redness of his skin and the jittery movements.

Not that I was against drinking, I had just not done it for a while and was as healthy as I had been in years on my raw food lifestyle. He did not have anything else on for the day so I offered to take him for a drive. It was a lovely day and I enjoyed some company after a year of grieving the end of my marriage.

Pretty soon we were seeing each other every day. He used to joke to people how we met—had coffee and literally moved in together. And it was a little bit like that. Exactly. Charles talked a lot about his ex-wife. I found myself counselling him. I would jump out of bed in the morning, make a green smoothie for us, singing in the kitchen and he would say, "God, you're so nauseatingly happy. Can you at least wait until I've had a coffee?"

I was happy and I wanted him to be happy too. I tried to do what I could to help him smile. He was quite deep and a sad person at times. He seemed to find comfort in talking about all the drama in his life.

We would walk on the beach in the mornings and he would hardly utter a word to me and then go off on his own picking up stones. When he did talk about what was going on, it was usually about how awful his ex-wife was and how she had treated him so badly. I was there for him to talk it all out, listening and being there for him. I noticed that we never talked much about me. Another red flag. I had told him about Harry and the story behind it and said that he was the first man I had been with since Harry and wondered if I could fully trust again. I asked Charles to please be careful with my heart and just be honest with me.

I introduced him to raw food, healthy eating and, of course, a lot more of Bikram yoga. When I first went to his house and looked in his fridge, all that was in there was some cottage cheese and a bottle of Chardonnay. That pretty much said it all about how he was living before he met me. I helped him turn all that around and before long he was looking really well and healthy and feeling great.

I, on the other hand, started to decline. My mood started to get more depressive. I wasn't the chirpy little budgie he had called me when he first met me. It was almost like he was becoming me and I was becoming him. The dramas continued in his life and I was always there to listen. I noticed him paying a lot of attention to females: female students, female teachers and even walking on the beach. I wondered if that was my insecurity, having went through what I did with Harry. I did mention it to him, but that was probably the worst thing I could have done because from then on, he played on it. We would walk on the beach and he would say, "She's lovely. Oh, she's got a lovely smile." Someone else would walk by and he would say, "She's got beautiful skin." And this went on continuously until, I wondered if he was actually trying to get a reaction out of me.

Later, I came to know that he was, but then I was so confused by this behaviour. Even with my female teachers. One teacher got more than a few comments: "I really like Sally," he said one afternoon.

"I know, she's a lovely girl," I replied.

He said, "I really, really like her."

"Yes, I know, you've told me three times, Charles," I said, trying not to react.

One night after being out, Charles had had quite a bit to drink. I was getting ready for bed and he was in bed and said to me, "I really like Sally." Again, I thought. Why does he keep doing this?

And he said, "Sally, Sally, Sally, Sally, Sally, Sally, Sally, Sally."

"What on earth are you doing?" I asked, perplexed. I tried so hard not to get angry, but it was really hurtful. When I look back on this now, I think I was pretty stupid not to just walk out right then. When you've been hurt and abused and betrayed as I was in my marriage, it's so easy to doubt yourself. I think I put up with things that I would never normally put up with because of the brokenness that I experienced after my marriage.

Before long I started to react to these little games, which was exactly what he wanted. He seemed to get something out of the drama. I wasn't used to fighting like this. I hardly fought with Harry until the end of our marriage. I found myself getting anxious and becoming nervous and fearful. It was like my energy was being drained from me. When it was good, it was so good. We had lots of laughs, passion, we travelled well together, but when it was bad, it was very, very bad. Sometimes he would not speak to me for three or four days. Passing me in the hallway, ignoring me. I was left wondering what I had done. Then he would just start talking to me again. He told me once that he sometimes did not talk to his ex-wife for three weeks and his children had to pass messages between them.

One day, visiting his mother, she told me that his father had been extremely cruel to her. That he'd had an affair with someone in the ballet. She said it was terrible living with him. He was so cruel. Right then I realised that if I stayed with this man, I would end up just like her. Bitter and angry, having been abused and treated cruelly.

As time went on, I noticed that I was feeling very suspicious of him. I really had a feeling he was having an affair. But when I asked him about that, he denied it and said I was being stupid because I was so damaged from the breakup of my marriage.

On New Year's Eve, I sent a text to all of my friends in my phone, saying Happy New Year. One response was from an ex-boyfriend of mine. It wasn't a very nice response. It was quite cheeky and a little bit rude. And Charles went berserk. I had never seen this jealousy in him before. But it lasted for about three days. He made out that

New Boyfriend

I had done something to entice the ex-boyfriend and no matter how much I explained to him that I had just sent a text to my group, a group text, he was very suspicious. He had asked me to join him on a trip to Malta that was coming up for his business, but when the trip got closer, there was no mention about me going. This made me even more suspicious.

When he was away, I tried to have little contact with him just to think about what to do in this relationship. One day he texted me and called me Jenny. I flew off the handle and texted back, "Why are you calling me Jenny? Who's Jenny?"

And he said, "Oh, don't be silly. I don't know why I called you Jenny, I meant to call you Norma."

Looking back at all these shenanigans, these are some of the games that narcissists play.

I flew to Bali to run a health retreat and he was in Europe, supposed to be in France, and was going to meet me after. Initially he was going to come with me, but I thought it best that he join me after the retreat so I could stay focused. The day after he arrived, one of my students said to me, "Norma, I have never seen you like this. What has happened to you?"

I was a mere shadow of my shining self. I felt weak, vulnerable, anxious. I really didn't know what was wrong with me. But it was a place that I went to very often in this relationship.

Meanwhile, back in yoga land, things were getting very strained with my landlord. My lease had expired and he refused to sign a new lease unless I paid a very substantial increase in rent. I was not prepared to do it and could not do it. My health was really taking a turn for the worst. My energy levels were so low. I felt sad so much of the time; between the landlord and Charles, things were just getting more and more stressful. I soldiered on as I had always done, but it was getting more and more difficult. As the landlord refused to sign a lease, I decided to close the school down and look for somewhere else, which I did.

During the time the studio was closed down I spent a lot of time in bed. I was very sad and depressed. I really didn't know what to do. I looked around to try and find another space, but all my money had been put into that studio.

One day, lying in bed, feeling really flat, I had a flu and I thought maybe I'd go and visit Laura in Melbourne. I called her up to see how she was going and she wasn't good at all. She told me that she had been to what she called a retreat facility. Which had turned out to be a drug and alcohol rehab. She seemed to be ashamed to tell me but I thought it was a step in the right direction for her. She said that she was getting better but still struggling.

I didn't mention where I was at and felt that it was inappropriate to talk about my sadness when she was having such a difficult time. So I didn't mention going to visit her in Melbourne. And we had a nice chat and I said that I would call her in a week or so to see how she was going. A week or so later, I got a message from a girl that worked with Laura and I in Melbourne. I was very surprised to hear from her because I hadn't really been in contact with her since I left Melbourne. The minute I heard her voice on the message machine, my stomach sank. I knew something was wrong.

Charles happened to call from London where he was, in between me getting back to the friend, and I said, "Something's wrong with Laura. Something's really, really wrong."

He said, "You don't know that yet. Call your friend back, find out what's happened."

But I could feel it. Something happened so drastically to my body that I went to the toilet and had diarrhoea. I plucked up the courage to call my friend in Melbourne and the news was not good.

"Hey, Cathy," I said. "What's going on? How did you get my number? What's wrong?"

She was silent for a while and then she said, "We've lost her, Norma." I knew she was talking about Laura because that was the connection we had together.

"No," I shouted. "No … what's happened?"

She had hung herself. I couldn't breathe. Laura had four children. The youngest girl had found her hanging in the lounge room. All I could say was, "No, no. No, she can't do this. No, she can't do this."

Cathy was sobbing. I was sobbing.

"But why? Why would she do this? Why would she do this?" I said to Cathy.

It turned out she had some financial problems and was drinking again. Laura and I had talked about this. I had urged her to sell her house as I had mine. Even though I didn't own my house anymore I was still out of debt at this point. And I urged her to do the same, but apparently the shame she felt was beyond anything that we could imagine.

I walked around numb for days, shaking my head. It also brought back to me the attempted suicides that I had had previously. Thinking about the pain that it would have caused if I had been successful, like the pain that myself and all of Laura's family and friends were now suffering.

I have often said that no one can really understand suicide unless they've been to that place. The pain is so great that you really can't see a way out. Today I work with a lot of people that have had suicidal ideation, and severe depression. And when I'm able to share my story that I too have had those same feelings and been to that dark place, it somehow helps them. I wish so much that I could have helped Laura. One thing that I've experienced when I was in those dark places is that you really believe that no one can help you. And this is obviously the place that dear Laura got to.

I received a phone call from my lawyer telling me that the landlord had agreed to let me pay by the month at a decent rent, if I would come back. He was still not prepared to give me a lease, but he was prepared to let me back in at a lower rent rate. During this time the local paper had done an article on him, which apparently he had gone berserk about. It was about the landlords in our area charging extortionate rent rates and how it was really affecting the small businesses in our town. I'm not sure whether this had something to do with him agreeing to lower the rent to a decent rate, but I was happy to go back into the studio and start teaching again.

During this time I decided it would be best to sell the studio, so I put the news out there to see if I could find an interested party. I had quite a few people interested, but no one was prepared to pay the money that I wanted for the studio. One in particular came from Las Vegas and he was very keen. We had many chats on the phone talking about how we would go about it, what I wanted, and he was asking about the landlord. I told him about the issues that I had with the landlord and that he could be difficult, but he was still very positive about it. Then he changed his mind and decided it wasn't for him.

A few months later, I was teaching at the studio. One of my students came in with his stepson, who was a dancer in Las Vegas. And he just casually mentioned, "Oh, there's a chap in Las Vegas telling everybody that he's going to get the Bikram Yoga school in Byron Bay."

New Boyfriend

"That's not true," I said. "Nobody's buying the school here." And I thought it must've been about the person that was interested. Perhaps he was thinking about getting it, but of course he wasn't getting it. Meanwhile, the landlord was being more and more difficult. He asked me for $8,000. The $8,000 was for a bank guarantee. But I was not prepared to pay $8,000 for a bank guarantee when he wouldn't give me a lease.

Within 24 hours, I received notice to get out of the building within 28 days, unless I paid the $8,000. I really didn't have a choice, but I didn't have $8,000. He agreed on $5,000. Once he received the $5,000 he ripped up the notice, to my relief. But within 24 hours after that, he gave me another notice to get out within 28 days unless I gave him another $3,000.

I found myself standing in the bank, ready to take out $3,000 to give to him. And as I approached the teller, tears welled up in my eyes. I felt like I was in chains to this man. Something inside me said, "Enough." I did not withdraw the $3,000. Instead, I went to the studio and told my teachers that I would be closing down. I just couldn't live with this bullying anymore.

My health was going downhill faster every day, and I just didn't want to live like this. I asked one of my teachers to make the announcement because I was so upset I couldn't do it. Basically, the announcement was that by Friday we would have to get out. And that if they knew anyone that could help us move some of our things to a warehouse I had found, then all help would be welcome. Friday came around and there were people from everywhere. People with ladders, people with hammers. We pulled the walls down, ripped the carpets up, pulled the showers out, poured cement down in the showers. And we even saved most of the $20,000 mirrors which I was told would not be possible.

At one point, one of my students, who knew the landlord very well, came running and he said, "Norma, Norma, what are you doing?

What are you doing?"

"What does it look like I'm doing? I'm finished," I said.

"The landlord can't believe it. He's nearly having a heart attack," he said.

"Well, tell him he's fucked with the wrong person," I replied.

A couple of days before I had actually put everything together, I had called my lawyer and said to him, "Something fishy is going on."

"I know, Norma," he replied. My lawyer had worked out that there was some kind of deal going on between the guy in Las Vegas and the landlord. His intention was to get me out and let him take over my business. This wasn't going to happen.

I called the guy in Las Vegas and asked him what he was doing. He said, "Oh, I won't call it Bikram Yoga."

Because he would have called it Hot Yoga.

"I will rip everything out of that studio before I let you have it," I told him.

"You would not dare," he said.

"Fucking watch me," I replied, and hung up the phone.

And here we were, pulling things apart, putting things in skips, cleaning things up. People were there that I didn't even know. The place was back to the empty shell it had been before I had spent $200,000 on it. It was heartbreaking, but I knew that I couldn't go on the way I was with this landlord.

New Boyfriend

I had found a warehouse in the arts and industrial estate that was all old and tattered and filled with furniture, and the landlord there, a lovely human being, told me I could put my stuff there until I decided what to do. He also offered me the opportunity to set up another studio there.

One day I was at the doctor's, who was very concerned about me. I was telling her what I was feeling, what I was experiencing, and she said to me, "Norma, there are many things going on in your life that are very, very challenging. The worst for you, and I feel of most concern, is your relationship. You need to find a reason to want to live. What would make you feel better?"

I thought about all the things that seemed to be eroding my soul. "I want to go back to India," I replied.

CHAPTER TEN

Malignant Love

"The wrong person will give you less than what you're worth but that doesn't mean that you have to accept it."
                                              Sonya Parker

Things between Charles and I were getting increasingly unpleasant. I didn't really understand why there were so many arguments or silences. I had never experienced this in any relationship I had been in. To me, I'd much rather have a good old fight, get it over with, make love and move on. But this was agonising, not knowing why he was silent. Why he would make a cup of tea for himself and ignore me and go into his office and close the door. I really didn't understand this behaviour at all.

When he was ready to talk, he would come out as if nothing had happened. Give me a hug and act as if everything was fine. It was so welcoming for me to have him talk again that I didn't even mention it. There seemed to be a pattern of the silences and eruptions. The eruptions were usually caused by him doing something to stir me up or aggravate me, try to push my buttons. Especially when things were really good, when I was feeling really happy and maybe I had a really good day at the studio, there was always something he would do to try to bring me down.

But it became obvious, especially towards the end, that he was actually doing these things to trigger me. And when I was triggered, I was angry. And when he had a response from me, it made him feel alive. The bigger the response, the more alive he felt. He told me once that he had used a slingshot to hurt a little bird when he was a little boy. The little bird fell from the tree, and he ran to rescue it. Put it in a box and tried to save its life. Apparently, it died in the end. There were many times that I felt like that little bird who had fallen from the tree due to his slingshot.

In public he was a pure gentleman. People thought he was just perfect for me. He was handsome, intellectual, articulate, very gentle, very kind. Or so I thought. Years after we separated, a friend from Melbourne who had had dinner with us said, "Thank God you got rid of that one, Norma."

"Why?" I said.

"He was an asshole. He was always putting you down."

"Why didn't you tell me?" I said.

"You can't do that, girlfriend. You just don't do that."

I had to find that out for myself. All I wanted to do was go back to India, be in the ashram, sit with my guru and listen to his wisdom.

Malignant Love

On my previous trip to India, I had met a couple who had introduced me to another guru. I completely fell in love with this being as soon as I saw him. He looked like Moses, and some of the disciples believed he was the reincarnation of Moses. Or other people saw him looking just like Santa Claus. A combination of both, I thought. He had a wicked smile. Amazing sense of humour. Was highly intelligent. And I had never heard such wisdom as I had from this guru. It was almost like a magnet when I met him. I wanted to go back again and again. It turned out that I had, in the end, visited India six times in three years. That's how strong the magnet pull was with him. Four of those times were with him.

Before I knew it, I was on a flight heading back to India again. The other disciples were becoming like family. Some of them I would meet regularly. Some were new each time I went. The guru taught us Kriya Kundalini Yoga, which I so desired to teach. I would meditate for hours in the ashram. Doing the Kriyas, the chants, sitting with him in satsang listening to his wisdom. At the end of the week, I had made a very clear decision. I did not want to open another studio. Three were enough. To be honest, one was enough.

When I returned, I discussed my decision with Charles.

"You can't do that," he said. "People rely on Bikram yoga. People rely on you. Your teachers rely on you for a job. Your students rely on you. Many of them are sick. And now your new landlord is relying on you so that he and his wife can retire."

I had a friend in Noosa who was in the process of opening her second studio. I'd contacted her and suggested that I come and help her. She was thrilled. I also offered to sell all of my equipment to her to put into her second studio. She was going to come to Byron to have a look at everything, and we were going to go ahead with this deal. I would have sold everything to her and been way ahead financially.

I went to the warehouse to have a chat with Archie, the landlord. Archie was a kind and gentle man who loved to stay healthy. He was extremely well mannered and had a kind sparkle in his eyes. When I walked into the warehouse the smell of dust made my eyes and nose itch. Archie was extremely pleased to see me, as he always was. He came and gave me a hug and started telling me how excited he was about the opportunity of me starting a business in his building so that he could retire. I couldn't say anything about not opening another studio within his building. I asked to have a look at my stuff and walked through the big, old, cluttered building. Cluttered with my furniture. Cluttered with his furniture. Archie was a little bit of a hoarder. His wife was looking forward to me encouraging him to start clearing some things out. I sat down on one of the old dusty couches that belonged to Archie, put my head in my hands, and started to cry. I just didn't want to do it again.

That night I was very clear as I was speaking to Charles about what I had decided to do. We'll move to Noosa. I'll start anew up there. I'll start a raw food business. Again, he reminded me of my responsibility, what I had started here in Byron Bay and how it was really important that I continue it for the people.

"No," I said. "I'm ready for change."

The next day we went to the warehouse together. Archie was moving around some furniture, showing me how much he had already moved out of the building. Very excited and wanting to know when I could start. He promised he would get the rest of the stuff out by a certain time so that I could start building. On the tip of my tongue, it was there: "Archie, I've decided not to open another studio. I'm just not well enough. I just don't have the energy. I just don't have the funds." With the excitement in his eyes and the pressing feeling of Charles's judgement, before I knew it, I was agreeing to open another studio. As I got in the car, Charles looked at me and said, "So you've decided to do it then?"

Malignant Love

"Yes," I said. "I just can't let them all down."

This was to be one of the biggest mistakes I had ever made in my life. It was another case of not listening to my intuition. Every cell in my being was telling me not to open that studio. But I just couldn't let people down. The landlord, the teachers, the students. Somehow I felt they were all my responsibility. And very soon I was organising builders, painters, and was renovating the building with very little funds. I managed to borrow some here and there. I used a credit card, organised the payment plans, organised free memberships for people who were helping on the weekends. And on Easter Sunday, I opened my fourth studio. I called it The Resurrection. There were 43 people in the class that day. Some very excited students to finally have their yoga again. It was a much more humble version of the beautiful studio that I had pulled apart. But the students loved it. They were happy. They loved the outdoor shower, which was resurrected from my old house in Billinudgel. A lot of it was resurrected. It was a good name, The Resurrection.

I decided that once the studio was up and running, it would be a good idea for me to sell it. At one point, I did put it on the market, but didn't get the interest I was looking for. So I kept going. My energy was running out. I would drag myself in to teach a class and drag myself out. Going home wasn't really pleasant because there was always something going on with Charles. I couldn't understand why I could just not leave him.

One day I received a call from someone from my past telling me that Paul, my boyfriend of six years, had died. I was in shock. Completely heartbroken. Paul was a beautiful man and shared a really special part of my life. His sister-in-law called me and said, "Norma, there are no photographs. There're no other photographs since you left."

I had boxes of photographs of us. I offered to pull them out and send them for the funeral. As I was going through the photographs, something really hit me. I was looking at photographs of Paul and I. A much younger version of me smiling. I had joy in my eyes. My dimples were huge. He always had his arms around me. He obviously really loved me. Paul was Scottish. His parents were Scottish. I felt like part of the family for the six years I spent with him. And we stayed in touch right up until he died.

What on earth was I doing with this man Charles? There was absolutely no love from him. In fact, in the whole time I had been with him, he had never told me that he loved me. Looking at these photographs really made me wake up. I was trying to get the photographs scanned and into the computer to send to Sydney, but I didn't know how to use the scanner. Charles, who was very computer savvy—that's what he did for a living—wouldn't help me. I sat there for two and a half hours until I worked it out. And then he casually said as he walked by, "Oh, you managed to send them then."

After Paul's funeral, I came back to Byron knowing that I had to end this relationship. I knew I didn't want to be with this man. I knew that I deserved to be with someone who did love me. I just couldn't work out why my energy was so drained. Why I didn't have the strength to just tell him to go. Normally, if I didn't like something, I had no problem telling someone. I just couldn't work out why I was finding it so hard to leave this relationship.

Charles had returned after his trip to Malta. He told me that his phone wasn't working when he was there, so we really didn't have a lot of contact during this trip away. But I really wasn't bothered, because in my mind I was trying to work out how to end the relationship. He mentioned something on one of the few phone calls that it might be an idea for him to move out in January. I was quite happy with that. That was the best thing, in my opinion.

During his time away, I had a birthday party with quite a few friends. I was dressed up and was having a wonderful time. And I put some photographs on Facebook of the very special night. The next day he was on the phone telling me how beautiful and happy I looked. And how he missed me. Nothing was said about him moving out in January. When he returned, his suitcase was lying in his office for a week, unopened. I wondered when he was going to open it and let me do some washing. He never did the washing, or the cleaning, or the dusting, or the vacuuming, or the cooking. I did everything in the home.

After a week, he was heading out to the dentist. I arrived home after teaching a class, and the suitcase was open. I decided to go through and pull his things out to wash them. On the very top of all the clothes was a book of poetry, which I'd never seen before. I opened it up and read the words inside written by hand. "My darling Charles, love is our Graceland." My heart nearly stopped. It was from Jenny. Inside the book was a receipt ... a receipt for Victoria's Secret lingerie. I had received a vegan cookbook for my birthday with no "love". Just "I hope you enjoy" written inside. Someone called Jenny had received lingerie from Victoria's Secret. Beside this receipt was a receipt for a hotel in Portugal the previous year. The date on it was from the week before he had met me in Bali. No wonder my energy was drained, as my student had pointed out. He had been having sex with Jenny then went straight over to Bali to do the same with me.

It was very obvious to me that he wanted me to find these. I sat on the chair with my heart in my throat, pounding.

"Right," I said out loud. "Show me the truth. Show me the truth. Show me the truth. What else? What else is there to see?"

And the little voice in my mind said, "Computer."

"No," I replied out loud again. "He keeps his computer locked. There won't be anything in the computer."

Undercover Angel

Again, I heard "Computer".

So I opened the computer, and for the first time ever it wasn't locked. It was open. And there was a plethora of emails between Charles and Jenny. I could hardly breathe as I was reading the words. They were planning for him to move to where she lived. She was talking about a yoga school, "just around the corner, my darling, so that you can go to your beloved yoga." One of the emails was a picture of her breasts.

It was the strangest feeling ever. Something inside of me felt calm. It was as if, thank goodness, I now knew the truth. At the same time, my hands were trembling as I read the email. Here I was, realising my biggest fear. Probably reliving the pain of Harry and so many other previous partners. I went out, bought a packet of cigarettes, smoked two and sat in the lounge room waiting for Charles.

When he came in, he looked happy. And I looked at him and said, "Who's Jenny?"

"Oh, don't start all that again," he said patronisingly. He was referring to the phone call when he was in Malta, when I told him that I had a very, very strong feeling he was having an affair and his answer to that was, "I will not dignify that with an answer."

That's what he was referring to when he said, "Don't start all that again."

"Do you want me to go and open your computer and show you the emails I found? Give it up, Charles. Enough games," I said calmly.

He sat down on the couch beside me and told me she was an ex-girlfriend from many years ago. She had contacted him out of the blue, which I really didn't believe.

But it didn't matter anyway. This was a chance for me to get out of this relationship.

"Did you at least use a condom?" I said.

I could tell by his look that he hadn't.

"You disgust me," I said. "And you had the cheek to talk about Harry because he went to prostitutes. At least they use condoms. You disgust me. You're lower than pond scum, and I want you to leave."

"It's my house too," he said. "I'm on the lease."

"I want you to fucking leave," I said. He went to the bathroom, threw up, came out, looked at me and said, "I love you" for the first time in our two-year relationship.

CHAPTER ELEVEN

Empath and Narcissist

"Going through a breakup with a narcissist is its own special kind of hell on earth."

— Unknown

For the next few weeks, there were a lot of emails and phone calls from Charles; some I took, some I didn't. He begged me to go see a therapist. He begged me to see if we could work things out. I was very clear that this was not going to happen.

One night, I was having dinner with a girlfriend, and I received a text from him on the way home, except this text wasn't actually meant for me. Or was it? It was supposed to be for Jenny. These were some of the games that he would play to try and get some reaction out of me. Before I understood what games he played, I lost my power completely. It came to my mind that he was still in contact with Jenny, even though he was trying to get back with me. I decided to let her know, so I copied and pasted many of the emails he had sent to me and forwarded them on to Jenny. I told her that she could have him, that he was a narcissistic, selfish, twisted person and I wanted nothing to do with him.

The next day, I received an email from him saying, "How dare you upset my friend?"

I assumed that she had ended the relationship. So here he was now with no one, no one to feed off energetically, which is a very difficult place for a narcissist to be.

I threw myself into researching and studying narcissism. I really had to understand what had just hit me. Even though I had ended relationships before and had been extremely heartbroken, I hadn't ever felt as energetically depleted as I did with the ending of this relationship. It was like my life force had been sucked from me. The more I studied narcissistic abuse, the more I realised that that's exactly what had happened to me.

Learning about all the different terminologies in the narcissistic abuse forums, I realised that I was a victim of most of them, even when he was trying so hard to get back with me, what they call hoovering me back into his web. He even used a friend of mine to do what they call abuse by proxy. I would receive lengthy emails from him explaining how much he loved me, how much he wished things had been different, how I had been an important love in his life, and how I had changed his life in so many positive ways. I mostly didn't respond to the emails, but sometimes I was hoovered back in, as they say, and I would respond. The minute I responded, I felt weak. I lost my power. I had no energy for days, and I wouldn't hear from him for days after I had responded. Then I would pull back, get stronger, and then I would hear from him again. It was like a dance of energy or a dance of battle between the energy.

The more I learned about narcissism, the stronger I got. I realised that so many of the times where he had accused me of certain feelings were actually his feelings that he had been projecting on to me. This is one of the things that narcissists do. Not only are they projecting their unwanted energies into you, they're also pulling energy from you. The no contact was very difficult on an energetic level. I just couldn't understand why sometimes he would just all of a sudden come into my mind and I would be drained of energy and feeling weepy. One day, I was standing in the kitchen making a chocolate cake, singing, feeling quite joyful, and all of a sudden, this wave of regret came through my being. The tears started to pour down my face. I started to shake. And in my mind, I heard my voice saying, "It's not yours. Go and cord cut."

I had learned to cord cut through some of the forums I had been on, which had been quite helpful but didn't seem to last for a long time. I decided to cord cut and see if my feeling was any different. This regret that was pouring through me, would it still be there? I lay on the bed, closed my eyes, and did the cord-cutting process, and I sat up upright, wiping the tears from my eyes thinking, what the fuck was that? Because it wasn't mine.

As soon as I had done the cord cutting, there was no feeling of regret. There was no sadness. There were no tears. But what I did see in my mind was a vision of Charles looking at photographs of us together and him feeling regret. And this was coming into my field from the other side of the planet because he was now living in Europe.

As I learned more about the games that narcissists played, I was able to defend and protect myself. But it took about six months just for the games to stop, the emails to stop. Our last meeting was in a coffee shop in Bangalow, where we used to have breakfast. He had been in Byron for a few days and asked to see me. He told me where he would be for breakfast, lunch and dinner and asked me to join him when I wanted to. I ignored the emails and the invites. Until a friend texted me and told me that she had bumped into Charles and she thought he may have changed. That was enough to send me into self-doubt and I agreed to meet him in the coffee shop we had often went to. That was the last time I ever saw Charles; I must have needed to get one more kick up the backside. He was still playing games and in touch with Jenny. I later found out that he had gone into my emails and deleted those last few emails where he was asking to meet up. He was probably scared I would send them on to Jenny. My last email to him said, "Don't ever contact me again, don't phone me, don't email me, don't text me, I SEE YOU."

Then I put a quote:

"In the end, only three things matter: how much you loved, how gently you lived, and how gracefully you let go of things not meant for you." – Buddha

And added… "It took me a while to get the last one."

There were so many games being played. Thankfully, I was able to stay away after his last visit. It was extremely painful and confronting. But somehow, I must have needed that to get brought to my knees one last time.

I had made an appointment with a well-known clairvoyant a few months before but she had a long waiting list. It turned out that my appointment was confirmed with seemingly perfect timing, just as Charles and I had broken up. I drove to Brisbane to meet with her and she helped me understand a lot about the situation I was in. She was no fluffy 'love, trust and pixie dust' kind of reader. There was no telling me what I wanted to hear, but her advice gave me strength.

"You really have been through the wringer and I can see you have been to hell and back," she said.

The tears started to roll down my face and she went on: "You can't do what you came here to do, Norma, when you're in a place of struggle and don't have the energy for other people when it's all about having resilience for yourself.

"The good news is that you have an incredible capacity to heal, Norma, not just physically but emotionally and psychologically. Life is just not going to break you. And I know it feels like you're broken, but you're not. That is the great strength of you, that you can just bounce back from just about anything.

"The bad news is that you have massive adrenal fatigue; I'm really concerned about that. Are you under the care of anyone, is anyone looking after you? This is almost all from stress. There are no pathogens to cause this but the chemical cascade of being worried, in your head and feeling massively unsupported."

"No," I replied with a lump in my throat. "I'm on my own."

"What I'm concerned about, Norma, is that you have lost your connection to your own personal practice, you give so much dynamic change to so many people but it's at such a big price in you currently," she continued.

She then gave me some guidance about the best foods to eat, advising me not to eat anything that came from cruelty because my body would feel it, and moved into my spiritual lessons.

It was an hour and a half session so I will not be able to cover everything here. She said that the thing I came here to learn in this life was to listen to my own judgement and to be able to do that I needed time on my own and to listen to what my heart tells me.

Nicole has the ability to see the colours in your aura and explain what the colours mean. Some of the colours are given to us and some we choose. About 5% of the population have master colours and they are very rare and you don't choose them for yourself, they are given to you. It's unusual to have a master colour and Nicole found that I have three. To receive master colours, you have to be an old soul and have reached a level of self-awareness and spiritual awareness. You need to have chosen a purpose which is about service to others and the universe gives you the master colours and a gift for you to further your purpose. Everyone with a master colour, from a very early age, has a sense that they are meant to do something.

"I want to explain your aura, Norma, as it's magnificent and now I know why your life is so hard," Nicole said. "The first thing I want to explain to you is that you have what is called a 'psychic channel'; only about 2% of the population have this and it was given to you. This looks like a big, white funnel that plugs you directly into the universe. That's why you will know the right thing to say, the right thing to do to motivate someone. You don't know why you know it, you just know it. It's wide open in you, Norma, but it's not working very well because you're exhausted. You're really a wise old elder, Norma, and it gets easier when you get older for people to believe you but most of what you know goes against the grain, so it can be a lonely path."

The next master colour, she explained, was the purple colour on the outside of my aura. She laughed that this colour had been hijacked by the new age movement but is the rarest of colours.

"You've had this colour for more than one lifetime, Norma, and you've earned it. Purple is the colour of the spiritual guru. It's that sense of 'I don't need to be here anymore but I've arrested my journey and I will not go further because I'm here to be an agent of transformation.'

"It is such a hard colour to live with. I'll tell you why; it's like being a PhD in a class full of kindergarten students. When you have come here as a teacher, there needs to be a distance between you and your students. You have to accept that it is going to be lonely and if you can find one, two or three people in your whole life who understand you and support you then hang on to them because I'm telling you that the majority of people in the world just won't be able to meet you where you are and there is no ego associated with that. If you're a PhD in a classroom of kindergarten students, some of them will probably eclipse you one day when they grow up but they're not there now. You've come here as an agent of transformation for people, groups or the planet and it's a tough gig and it also means everyone you'd really relate to isn't here, they're all over there! And the hard thing is that you don't need to be here but you look down and go 'shit, what a mess, well, I can help' and you come back in, but you don't come in with a bounding sense of joy, you come in with a deep breath, grit your teeth and let's do it all again. It means you cannot help but be a teacher and you're right at the leading edge of things. You know the saying, 'you can't be a prophet in your own town'? So most people who have purple need to move away from family and friends."

Nicole went on to explain the third master colour and five chosen colours before talking about my soul's obstacles.

It was an incredible reading and gave me much insight about my life. I sometimes listen back to that reading and continue to learn from it. One thing she was very clear about was my relationship with Charles.

"Stop wondering if you've done the right thing about this relationship, Norma," she sternly advised. "It's a burning building; GET OUT OF THERE! and know that you will be stepping into a magnificent relationship but you have to get yourself sorted. You'll never meet this person in the mess you're in now."

The last thing I was interested in was another relationship. I was still trying to understand the train wreck that hit me.

What is this dance between empaths and narcissists? My relationship with Charles encouraged me to really study this phenomenon in depth. I had no doubt in my mind that I was an empath. An empath is someone who takes on the feelings of others, not just feels compassion, but takes the feelings into their own body. I was a physical and emotional empath. That means that when I sit next to someone I can feel their emotions in my own body. This is actually a gift for a healer. But unless you are aware of it, it really feels like a curse. And for most of my life, I was not aware of it. So, this is why the warnings that I had at other times in my life were there. They were all telling me the same thing. The warning from the elder, the Reiki teacher and other healers that I had been to, all telling me the same thing about something that I did. What they were telling me was I was an empath.

Not to be confused with highly sensitive people: all empaths are highly sensitive people, but not all highly sensitive people are empaths. A highly sensitive person may be sensitive to lights and sounds and even people, but they don't necessarily take in the emotions of others to their physical being. And empaths that are unconscious of what they are doing can become very, very ill. This is why Papa K told me if I didn't take care of myself that I could end up like him, as he was in a wheelchair. This is exactly how I felt at the end of this relationship, completely wiped out, completely deleted.

But there's a lesson to be learned in everything. In all animals, there are a percentage that are empaths. Their job is to warn the rest of the pack of the dangers ahead or dangers that they sense. So, the empaths in this world also have their role to play in warning the rest of them or the rest of us. An empath has no problem expressing their feelings. In fact, it's one of the attractions to the narcissist, as the narcissist buries their feelings so deep that they're not even aware that they're there, and hence they project them onto the empath, who, without knowing that it's not their emotion, will express it.

For an example, if a narcissist has a buried feeling of inadequacy, which most of them do, they will project that onto the empath. The empath will then take the energy into their body and feel it as their own. And because they have the ability to express that emotion, they will express it as their own and deal with it accordingly. So in a sense, the empaths are the transmitters of the darkness. This is why the cord cutting didn't work for long periods of time because I was sending back the energy to the narcissist. They would only send it back to me as narcissists do to the empath. I had to learn to transmute the energy, which I already had a blueprint for but had no idea how to do it.

I believe that all empaths have the ability to transmute energy. But until we learn how to do that, we can be sick, depressed, emotionally imbalanced and living in isolation because we can be completely overwhelmed.

Dolores Cannon talks about the three waves of volunteers that have come here to raise the frequency of the planet. When I read this, I completely identified with one of the first wavers. The first wavers are the way showers or path cutters. They're the ones that take the first step through the denseness of this planet. Many of the first wavers have attempted or even succeeded in suicide. They find it extremely hard to be here. Having come from a frequency of a much higher vibration, they feel so out of place on this planet. That's exactly how I've always felt. And when I read about the first wavers, it was almost like, ah, somebody knows who I am, and Nicole's reading helped me understand this.

I'm not in any way saying that the volunteers are any better than anyone else here, but we have come here with an ability to raise frequency, and I believe that part of that is by transmuting the energy of the darkness. This is why the narcissistic people are attracted to us. So we can be victims and keep blaming the narcissist and never healing ourselves or anyone else, or we can understand our role and our mission here is to assist the planet by transmuting this darkness. That's when we really, truly step into our power and can make a difference.

The breakup with Charles left me so depleted, I struggled to get into the studio. My classes were less energetic, I had little energy to mentor the teachers. The electricity bills were getting higher and higher. I was in dispute with the current electricity provider because I couldn't believe that the bills were more in summer than they were in the winter when I hardly used the heaters in the summer due to the intense heat in Byron Bay. There was no winning against the electricity companies. In fact, one time they went into my bank account without my permission or my knowledge and took $5,000. It was at Christmas time.

My car was repossessed. And when they came to pick it up, instead of being angry, I was grateful because of the money I was paying every month for this car. The bills were coming in. And all I wanted to do was just close the doors and go to bed for a year. Instead, I headed back to my sanctuary in India.

The night of Shivaratri came. It was the big celebration in the ashram, and I was feeling very unwell. I had pain in my stomach, pain in my heart, sadness in my eyes. Shivaratri, as previously mentioned, is the night that you can ask for whatever you want from the Lord Shiva. I sat in the celebrations and prayed. Please show me. Am I on the right path? Am I doing the right thing? Why is my life so difficult? Why is my life so hard? Maybe I'm on the wrong path. Just show me. Just show me. Help clear my doubts and path to God, that's all I want.

The next day, we had a free day in the ashram and someone suggested that I go to see the Nadi leaf readers. I had read about them and was so excited to think that they might find my Nadi leaf. Of course, the rest of the Indian people laughed and said, "Ha, they'll never find your leaf. They haven't even found my leaf, and I'm Indian."

"Oh, well," I said. "I'm just keen to go and find out what it's all about."

One of my friends made the appointment for me. And before I knew it, I was heading off in a taxi to the Nadi leaf readers with one of my roommates and someone who was going to be able to translate what the Nadi leaf readers said.

When we got there, a little Indian man who didn't speak English at all came into the room and asked for my thumbprint and the first initial of my name. Then he went off and came back with two scrolls about 15 minutes later. These scrolls were so ancient that the papers were tattered and falling apart. These were called the Nadi leafs.

The story is that apparently 5,000 years ago, Shiva commanded that all souls on the earth have a record of all their lifetimes; these were written on palm (Nadi) leaves, an account of each soul. It is said that the Nadi leaf is only there for the people that seek out their leaf. So with the two scrolls under his arm, he showed me into a room. My friend, the translator, came too. He explained that all I needed to do was say yes or no in reply to the questions . The questions were things like:

"Your father's name begins with S," and I would say "no."

"You live in a country that begins with E," and I would reply "no."

And as I said no, he would flick through the palm leafs again, and again, and again, and again until he had finished one scroll. The feeling in my heart was that he probably wouldn't find my leaf and the Indian disciples would be correct. Again, I wasn't Indian, as my friends had reminded me. Then he went through the second scroll.

More and more, I began to answer some of the questions with yes answers. "Is your father's name the name of a king?" asked the Nadi reader.

"Yes," I replied, feeling a little more hopeful.

"Does the country of your birth begin with an S?" he asked again.

"Yes," I replied, sitting more alert.

Then he said something that absolutely took my breath away.

"Your father's name is William. Your mother's name is Agnes. Your name is Norma. You were born on November 27, 1965 in the evening on a Saturday. You are a teacher of yoga. You have just been ordained by your guru. You have three brothers and one sister. They are all married. You are divorced. You live alone."

I could hardly breathe. How on earth was the name of my mother and father and all this information written on a palm leaf from 5,000 years ago?

He then told me to go away and come back in an hour. After lunch with my friends, I returned to the Nadi leaf reader to hear what was in store for me. There was no sugar-coating at all. He told me that I had been born underneath a very difficult planetary aspect and would suffer until the end of my life. Of course, there were pujas (prayer offerings) to do to soften the blow of this.

He told me that I was very talented and yet did not get paid what I should get paid for the talents that I had, that I was a teacher of yoga, and that I would teach health-related topics and receive recognition for my work. He told me I would follow my guru and teach his teachings, that I would hear the voice of God, that I would see God, and I would teach what I learned to others.

He also told me that I was being cheated. When he said this, I understood that it may be the debt collectors he was talking about, the ones that were chasing me for the electricity bills and the previous ones from my car before it was repossessed. He told me that he could do a puja to help me find out who it was that was cheating me.

He asked if I had any questions. I asked if I should see Charles again, and he said immediately, "No. If you go back to that person, he will only hurt you more. Anyway, there is someone coming into your life, a very, very good man this time," he assured me.

It seemed to be that my path was all about a spiritual path. I had been ordained to teach Kriya Kundalini yoga and had waited a whole year after the teacher training to be able to teach it. The day before, I had been lying in bed feeling very sick in the stomach. I had begged my guru to let me teach Kriya yoga, but for a whole year he'd said no. The night before the Shivaratri, I was lying in bed with my bellyache, and one of the disciples came in and said, "Norma, the guru says you're now ready to become a hamsacharia," which means 'soul teacher'. I pushed the pain from my bellyache aside and could not wait for my ceremony.

That evening, I showered and went out to the satsang, where my guru invited me up to the front of the stage, wrapped his cloths that he wore around his shoulders around me, and chanted in Sanskrit. And before he'd done so, he had mentioned to the rest of the group that I had displayed an immense amount of courage. As I sat on my knees before him and he chanted around me, I felt like I was coming home.

After the ceremony, I started to shiver. I'm not sure if it was energy or I was actually cold on the warm, balmy Indian night. I went back to my room to get a cardigan. And out of the corner of my eye stood a tall figure with a beard and white hair. I recognised him to be Sri Yukteswar, which was said to be the previous incarnation of my guru. He nodded his head at me as if to say "Finally." I had seen visions of this previous life with him where I had been far from obedient.

After the Nadi leaf reader was a long taxi drive back to the ashram. It was late in the evening, but satsang was still going on. I was hungry and was waiting at the kitchen for food when the guru shouted over to me.

"Did you get my transmission today?"

"No, guru," I replied. "I've been out to the Nadi leaf readers."

"Ah," he smiled. "Did he clear your doubts?"

Again, my jaw dropped. It was as if he had been reading my mind the night before when I had prayed to have my doubts cleared.

I had a feeling that magic was being used by the yogis. I even heard that some had the ability to put karma onto unsuspecting disciples. I asked the guru about magic.

"It's ALL magic," he replied. "It's just a case of whether it is being used for good or bad."

A few days later, it was time for me to leave the ashram. I waited to say goodbye to my guru, and he came out. He stood beside me and said to me, "You are very strong, very, very strong."

I asked him when my life would get better, and he said, "It's your karma. Accept it with fortitude. You're very strong. You're an individual soul." Then he told me something that I'm choosing not to share in this book, but maybe one day I will.

NB: In 2019 I was told to stop transmuting and send back the energy to those I was picking it up from. It appears that as of this time, it was necessary to stay in the highest frequency possible and others needed to learn to take responsibility for their own emotions. It was important for the empaths to hold this energy for the event about to unfold.

CHAPTER TWELVE

The Dismantling

"You must give up the life you planned in order to have the life that is waiting for you."

Joseph Campbell

On return from India my energy was even more depleted than before. To think of all the times that I had sat and meditated and my energy was less than before. It really didn't make sense to me. I was feeling more and more depressed and unwell.

My car was gone and I was having issues with the electricity company, and the stress of the debts that were hanging over my head was very difficult to deal with. I was encouraged to go and see a financial counsellor that was part of a government plan. It was one of the best things I did. This little man called Terry had a wealth of knowledge about the debts that people can accumulate, the problems they can have and whether bankruptcy is the right option.

For me, I wanted everything to stop and so I was prepared to consider bankruptcy. Terry asked me if I had support because he said that many people that go bankrupt tend to suicide and it was really important that I had support in my life if I was to make this choice.

When I told him that I had no support, he was very hesitant to encourage me to go ahead with the bankruptcy. He said, "Norma, how would you feel if you saw your students in the street and they had memberships with you that they had purchased and because of the bankruptcy they'd lost it?"

"I would feel terrible," I replied in horror at the very thought.

"These are the things you have to consider," he said.

I kept on struggling along. Terry was wonderful helping me keep the wolves at bay. When someone was abusive and turned up at my studio swearing, banging on the door and demanding money, I would call him in tears. He would take over, call the debt collection agency and put them in their place. They really had no right doing this. Some of the things that they do to try and scare you are just barbaric and not legal.

One of the things that is legal is the selling of your debts. If a debt collector realises that you don't have the money to pay the debt, they will then sell that debt on to someone else: another debt collector. You can be hounded, chased and harassed for a whole year by the vultures. This can include late-night phone calls, texts, emails. I even had someone stalking me on Facebook trying to get money. When they realise you don't have the money, they will sell the debt off to someone again. Perhaps the debt is $10,000; they will sell the debt for $5,000 . The new debt collector will start the procedure all over again, chasing you for $10,000 plus interest, and the whole cycle starts again. This can go on for years, as it did for me.

The Dismantling

One night, it was quite late and very dark, I was sitting in my pyjamas and someone came on a motorbike up the driveway and then started knocking on my door. I didn't have people knock on my door at that time of night, so I was quite alerted when I opened the door. I saw a rough-looking guy, almost like a biker, bald head, black leather jacket; he was quite scary to look at.

He said, "I'm here from such and such an electricity company." I better not mention their name, as much as I would love to.

I said, "Oh, I've tried to negotiate a payment plan with them, but they won't accept it and the problem is, I don't have the money to pay it."

"You look like a nice girl," he said. "Why don't you find yourself a nice man?"

I started laughing and said, "No, I've been down that road. I'll stick to myself and my dogs, thanks very much."

"Oh," he said. "I had problems with my wife too," and then he started to tell me his problems, which happened to me very often.

"I just don't have the money," I said. I opened the door wider, invited him in and said, "You can take anything that you like. I have no attachment to anything."

And he said, "Oh, we don't do that here in Australia. They do that in the UK but not in Australia."

I said, "I don't care anymore about things."

He said, "You know what? You seem like such a nice girl. I think it's time you had a break. I'll tell them that you've got nothing."

I said, "Well, that is the truth."

He said, "You know what? They're bastards," and off he went, back on his motorbike. He was the only nice person I dealt with from debt collection agencies.

I just felt more and more sick, unwell, tired every day. The guru had given me a puja to do after I told him that the Nadi leaf reader had said I was being cheated on. I gathered everything I needed for the puja and started to do it every day. He said to do it for two weeks.

Twenty-four hours after beginning the puja, I went to my studio. There was a class on and one of my teachers was teaching it. The computer had been left open and one of the conditions I had with staff is that they do not use my computer for personal use. But this was obviously not happening as there was an email open on the computer. The email was to a student who had an interest in buying the studio. I had clearly told the teachers that I was not interested in selling the studio to this person as he had proved to be dishonest to me. I was very clear about not giving him any information about the studio. This email that was left on the computer was to this particular student. It was from the teacher that was currently teaching the class.

It was basically telling him how the studio was going, what advertising I was doing, how many people were in the classes, how well or not well the studio was doing, basically giving away my information to the student. I was absolutely furious. I felt my trust had been absolutely taken advantage of. When the teacher came out of the classroom, I said, "What the fuck is this?"

She was clearly not expecting me to be there. More than anything it hurt; I just adored this girl and really didn't expect this of her. She mumbled something about trying to help me. I reminded her that I had clearly asked her not to give information to the student. I felt my trust had been betrayed and just couldn't have her working in the studio anymore after that. I asked her to go away and think about it and I would think about it and the next day I met her on the beach and said, "I just can't have you work with me anymore, I can't have people work for me I don't trust."

That night I was doing the puja. I was thinking, well, that's the person cheating me and at the same time there was a very heavy feeling of intuition in my gut that perhaps there was something much more going on that I had yet to discover. The day before the puja was to be completed, I was in the studio looking at the figures. The other teacher came out and I asked her why the figures didn't add up. I could see what she had put in the bank and I could see what was supposed to be taken that day. There was a big difference and I could tell by her reaction that something wasn't right. When I asked her the question, she was very, very anxious. That night I woke up at 1:00 in the morning, sat bolt upright and thought, oh fuck, she's been stealing. And 1:00 in the morning I went through to the computer and started looking at the figures in the bank. There was a big discrepancy.

I had not bothered to look too deeply into these figures in the bank because I trusted this girl. I felt that she was supporting me through the difficult time I was experiencing.

Boy, was I wrong.

The next day I called someone that I knew had worked in the government financial section and asked her if she would have a look at my figures.

"Of course, Norma," she said. "Send them over."

Later that afternoon I got a phone call. "Norma, are you sitting down?"

"No," I said.

"Well, you better sit down, darling, because you are being robbed blind."

There was thousands of dollars missing and according to the computer it looked like it had been going on for a year. There were memberships that had been given away for free. There were towels and mats that had been given away for free. The towel and mat money did calculate up to quite a lot each month. One of the memberships that was given away was to someone who helped me around the studio. I did give him free memberships and he did some building and tidying up for me from time to time. But what I noticed was the last few months he had been given free memberships but hadn't done any work for me and I hadn't approved it. So I called him just to make sure and just to find out what was going on.

"Hank, can you tell me if the staff have been giving you free memberships?"

"No, Norma," he replied. "I've actually been paying cash from my memberships."

It looked like the teacher had been pocketing this away as well. I found it so hard to believe that she would do this after everything I had done for her. I had the proof, but the proof wasn't enough to have her convicted, unfortunately. Because I went to the police and the police told me that unless I had absolute proof, that's a camera, perhaps a camera filming her stealing, that I would be dragged through court and she would probably get off. The policeman, after I told him what I had been through, said to me in a very sweet, gentle voice, "Sweetheart, if you've had a lot of stress in your life, you'd have to go through a lot more. If you choose to do this, I can guarantee she'll get off."

Sheila, who had helped me working out the finances, advised me to be very careful. She said, "You can't accuse people, even though we have this proof, because according to the computer, it's not solid proof because other people have had access to it."

The Dismantling

We decided to invite the teacher and to have a discussion. One of the other teachers, who was a dear friend and still is a dear friend today, asked her very bluntly, "Why did you do it? Why did you do that? Why don't you just give Norma the money back?"

It was very obvious with her reaction that she was guilty.

Sheila's advice to me was to shut my mouth because she knew how fiery I could be, which was no problem because I felt so gutted and just hit rock bottom. I couldn't say anything.

When Sheila and the other teachers left, I was left with Gill on her own and I said, "Why did you do it? Why would you do this to me after everything I've done for you, I've been like a sister or a mother to you."

And she said, "I know. I thought you had money."

A few years later I was on the beach and recognised a little dog as Gill's partner's. There was a lovely girl walking her. We got chatting and I picked up the little dog and cuddled her; she seemed to remember me. "How do you know BooBoo?" she asked.

"Gill used to teach at my studio," I replied.

"Oh," she gasped. "You're the one she stole all the money from. You know she stole thousands from my partner too?" She was the new partner of Gill's ex.

It turned out that Gill's now ex-partner had also been advised not to waste time trying to get the stolen money back as it was explained to be a long, tiring , stressful procedure that was rarely successful.

I may have looked like I had money because nobody knew the suffering that I was going through, of the car being repossessed or battling with the bills. I always paid the teachers before I did anything else, so nobody knew what I was going through. And she thought I had money and felt entitled enough to take what turned out to be thousands of dollars from me.

I really felt at this point I had nothing left to give. All I wanted to do was get out of that studio, get away from the students. Even the students were behaving very demandingly, wondering why the prices had been increased or why the classes had been changed or why this teacher wasn't here. I felt like every reason I had to create and open this last studio was biting me in the butt and reminding me of what a mistake I had made putting everybody before myself.

The teachers I cared about were stealing. The students were becoming demanding and ungrateful and the only thing that was a positive in my mind were the landlords, who were still kind and still supportive. I had nothing left to give. I fantasised about closing the studio down. Thankfully, before I had to do this, somebody offered to buy the studio. I thought it would have been one of the happiest days of my life to sell the studio, but I was still sick and too exhausted to feel any joy whatsoever. The first day the money was transferred a huge portion of it was given away to pay off debts. That was a relief. There were still more debts and more debt collectors to chase me.

A positive thing was that I had time to take care of myself. I was able to go to the doctor's and pay for the injections that I was getting and the herbs and the medicines and the vitamins to try and build up my strength. I was diagnosed with chronic fatigue syndrome, fibromyalgia and depression. As I now had no income coming in, I was encouraged by my counsellor to go to Centrelink, which was such a terrible thought. I had worked since I was 13 years old and the only time I had help was in Scotland at the age of 16 for six months in between school and college.

The fact that the manager of Centrelink was actually one of my students made me terrified of going. I remember feeling the most embarrassing shame I had felt in many, many years when I went there to claim Centrelink. She was so wonderful and kind and as I came out of the bathroom with tears in my eyes after sobbing, she took care of me like a sister.

All the people in Centrelink were just wonderful. I also had to see a counsellor within Centrelink and I said to him, "Oh, don't worry, I'll be working again. Within a few months."

He looked into my eyes and said, "Norma, it's going to take you a lot longer than a few months, my dear, to recover from what you've been through. You have to understand you have had a breakdown."

In my mind, I still thought I would be up and working and doing something else again within a few months. The hardest thing of all during this time was the battle I had in my mind about how I should be working, how I should be doing something. Even though I had worked since I was 13 years old, this was the first time I had ever not worked in my life. I found it really difficult, but my health made me realise I had no choice. There were days when I just spent the whole day on the couch and even to go into the kitchen and try and make some food was absolutely exhausting.

It was a very lonely time. I had nobody coming around and checking on me to make sure that I was okay. I had no family, I had no friends, I had no job anymore. I had no purpose. It was a very dark time of my life. My main focus was my dogs.

One night I was crying, sobbing in the foetal position, and I thought, how did I get here? How did I get here? From being happily married, having a successful business, a beautiful million-dollar house, to receiving money from Centrelink and struggling to get by. The voice in my head said, "Well, now, you're no longer Norma the teacher. You're no longer Norma the wife. You're no longer Norma with all the money and you're no longer Norma the friend. Now you will come to know who the real Norma is."

Everything that was transient was gone. I was left with a foundation that was shaky and this is what I realised I had to work on, from within, to truly learn who I was without all of those baubles and bangles, and it was no tea party nor for the faint-hearted. The yogis say this is the beginning of a true spiritual journey, everything preceding this is only the path towards it. The asanas, the meditation, are mere tools to arrive here. And who was here now? I thought. The Norma I believed had been dismantled? Was the pain over or just beginning?

CHAPTER THIRTEEN

Bikram's Fall Off the Pedestal

"Sometimes it's not the people who change, it's the mask that falls off."

Haruki Murakami

During my first few months after selling the studio, I wondered what I could do to try and make a living where I would be able to take care of myself and do something I loved. I came up with the idea to mentor some of the other Bikram yoga teachers, as this was something I had done for the last 10 years.

I was very good at helping teachers become better teachers. Most of that had to do with the fact that I had the ability to tell the truth.

And so, when their classes were not very good, I was able to tell them. I was also able to tell them how to make them good.

I had developed a reputation where people would call me and ask me to monitor their class and give them feedback. I had people come from all over the world to do this. I never charged, but gave of my time freely.

Some studio owners that I had initially mentored in their earlier years also would come back and say, "Norma, could you just take my class and tell me how I'm going, if I've slipped or if I need to get back on track?"

I would do so, sit down with them and write one, two, three, sometimes four pages of notes for them to go away and improve their classes. My new idea was to mentor the teachers from home. Sometimes I could even be in my pyjamas if I was having a very bad day, but I could listen to their class and I could tell them what needed to be improved.

Perhaps they were holding the postures too long. Perhaps they were addressing people inappropriately. Perhaps their voice was monotone and not very exciting, or they lacked energy. These are the kinds of things I would help people in the past with. I created the URL The Bikram Yoga Mentor, and was very excited that I could be doing something even though I was still very unwell.

Bikram was running a teacher training in Thailand and I decided to go along. I was still very unwell. It had been four months. I'd had lots of injections, and of course, lots of rest, but I was still unable to get through the day without having to nap.

When I arrived at the resort where the training was being held, I went into the restaurant. Bikram was sitting with his wife, Rajashree, and some other people. Rajashree spotted me and shouted, "Byron Bay, right? How are you?"

Bikram's Fall Off the Pedestal

She had visited me in Byron Bay a couple of years prior and I took her around the town and showed her my school. (This was before I had pulled it apart.) She was welcoming and lovely as usual.

"Sit down," she said. "Tell me how things are."

I sat next to Bikram and filled Raj in on what had been happening. Bikram quickly took over the conversation.

"I did a class last night ... look at me," he said as he pulled out his phone to show me photos of himself doing camel pose quite perfectly.

"Awesome, Bikram," I said.

It was like speaking to a little boy. Bikram did not seem to remember me; I had massaged him a couple of times when he came to Melbourne, once with two other therapists in his hotel room. That day I arrived before them. I had my aromatherapy oils all selected for a relaxing massage. As I was putting them into the mixing bowl, he said, "What is that?"

"It's your massage oil, Bikram," I said.

He smelled it and said, "Smells like shit! Add this," as he added some strong-smelling aftershave to my organic oils. I laughed my head off.

"Hey, come look what I bought," he said. He pulled out his shopping bags from an earlier spree.

"I don't spend a lot of money on clothes, you know, I'm smart." He smiled like the Cheshire Cat. "I buy one shirt that I like, and get my tailor to copy it and make twenty the same. Look at this," he said as he opened the box to a very expensive-looking watch sparkling with diamonds (or false ones ... who knew). "Is this not the most disgusting thing you have ever seen? You would not wear it if it was given to you as a gift, but I will wear it on stage." He beamed.

Stage, I thought. He really is performing out there. The girls arrived and he got his massage. The next time I massaged him alone at one of the yoga schools in Melbourne in between his teaching. I never felt any kind of sexual flirting from him at all. This was mainly the reason I found it hard to believe the accusations and the fact I had him on a pedestal.

The first class I took of Bikram's at the teacher training, I actually had to leave. I had only once left a class that was also Bikram's in Hawaii years before but I had gone back in after a drink. I had never sat down in a class before, so this was very difficult for me. I also found myself traumatised by the screaming that was going on from Bikram.

Bikram was being quite rude to people, especially teachers. One had been a teacher and mentor for nine years; he was screaming and shouting at him. I felt sick in the stomach. Later that day I met that teacher on the beach; he was so broken and sad and questioning his future with Bikram after that incident. My heart went out to him. Had Bikram changed so much? Or was I so naive I had just not seen it before? When I left the class I went back to my room to rest. It turned out that I had to be in the room for about 24 hours to recover as it had wiped me out so much. I was also unable to go to the lectures in the evening.

I was just too tired, but the main reason I had went there really was just to sit down with Bikram and tell him what my idea was, and not necessarily get his blessing because I didn't need to. It was really just to let them know what I was planning to do.

There were quite a few teachers who I knew at that time in Thailand on the teacher training. Some of them had worked for me and others were other studio owners. One in particular knew me quite well. We hadn't spent a lot of time together, but she knew of me and she knew my reputation in Australia as a mentor and a teacher who had a high respect for Bikram.

She had mentioned to me before on various phone discussions that my students were very well trained. Something wasn't right with this girl. I wasn't quite sure what it was, but one day I was sitting having lunch and she walked in with a group of the teachers and walked right by me and went and sat at a different table with all the teachers. I was quite perplexed as we had always sat together up until that moment.

One of the teachers who had worked for me came over to say hi and when I said, "Why on earth would you all go and sit at another table when I'm completely by myself?"

"Oh," she replied, "that's because Jane said you looked like you needed to be alone."

There were a couple of other things that alerted me to the behaviour of this particular studio owner. She was also receiving a lot of praise as the person who had brought Bikram yoga to Australia.

When this was discussed at a lunch table, I instantly looked at Jane. She knew that I knew she did not bring Bikram yoga to Australia because I knew the person that did. When she saw my look, she instantly corrected the rest of the table, who were all under the impression that she had brought Bikram yoga to Australia.

One day, I said to one of the teachers that worked for her, "What is it with this girl? Why does she behave so?"

And she said, "Norma, she's one of the most insecure women you will ever meet, and she's probably very threatened by you, you have such a great reputation as a teacher."

Well, she's not got any reason to be threatened by me," I said, "because I'm out. I don't want to have a studio anymore. I'm just going to do my own thing and help some teachers, so there's no reason at all to be threatened by me."

I had made a time to sit down with Bikram, just to talk about my idea. It just so happened that on the way to meet him, I had to share a buggy with Jane and another studio owner from Sydney, who I had never met before. By this time Jane was completely ignoring me.

I went in to meet Bikram and the other teachers were taken inside his villa, as I had requested to speak with Bikram alone. I sat down next to him and told him that I hadn't seen him for a few years because things had been very challenging for me.

I explained to him about the studios having to close down and relocate. I openly told him that I had been struggling personally, having had gone through a divorce, and financially. But in the end, I was happy to say that I had managed to save the studio and it was still running as Bikram Yoga.

He ushered me inside the villa where he was about to have a meeting with some studio owners. I said, "No, Bikram. I don't want to go in there. I'm not a studio owner anymore. I just wanted to talk to you."

"Come inside," he said. "Come inside."

He took me inside the villa, walked ahead of me, turned around, and as I hesitantly walked through the door, he pointed at me and said, very loudly, "I'm going to use you as an example of what a failure is! Look at her," he said to everybody in the villa, "she has lost four studios. She's a terrible businesswoman."

I could not believe my ears.

"I have not lost four studios, Bikram," I exclaimed. "I have only had to relocate a—"

"Shut up," he said, before I could even finish my sentence. "You're a smart ass." The other teachers just sat around and watched him tear me to shreds.

Within minutes, I was in hysterical tears. The strength in my body was completely drained. I had to sit down.

"Look at you," he said. "And now, you come to me crying. Why did you not come to me?"

"Bikram, I wrote to you," I breathlessly pleaded. "I wrote to Rajashri. She told me to write to you and you would help me. Nobody helped me. I was on my own with all of these challenges," I said.

Then Jane joined in. She piped up and said, "Oh, darling, I say this from my heart, but you had nothing to do with the other studio owners."

"That's rubbish," I said. "I mentored a large amount of those studio owners. What I didn't do was join in with the competition."

I had never agreed with competition and yoga and mine was the only school in all of Australia that refused to take part in the competition.

It had also turned out that Bikram had just stopped all competition because someone had accused him of sexual harassment.

"You should do what Jane does. If I say do competition, she does it. If I say stop competition, she does it. You should be like Jane."

"I don't believe in competition," I said. "It's not in my heart to combine yoga and competition and I would never ask my students to do anything that I don't believe in."

"You need a guru!" he shouted to me. "You're a failure. Why did you get divorced? Because you're a smart ass and didn't listen to your husband!"

Every time I tried to explain to him that, no, I had not lost four studios, I had opened four studios and had to relocate, but the two studios that I had founded in Australia were still running, he just wouldn't let me. And every time I did, I got cut off. The other studio owner who shared the buggy then joined the shaming party.

"Hey, you, you are being rude to boss. You need to respect boss. I mean, I love you, but you need to listen."

I said, "You love me? I met you five minutes ago. You know nothing about me."

It was very obvious to me that nobody was prepared to tell Bikram what they really thought, or perhaps they were that brainwashed that they thought it was all very fine what he did to me. He completely tore me to shreds, abused me, embarrassed me, humiliated me. After 10 years of devoting my life to this man. Jane knew this. She knew my reputation, and knew that I was probably one of the most loyal studio owners in Australia to Bikram.

Bikram was sitting next to me on the couch and someone asked him about Indian culture, and he said, "Well, you know, if I did this"—and he kicked me—"I would be disrespecting her."

He never called me by my name once. "And if I did this ..." and he kicked me again.

He kicked me three times to explain his story about Indian culture. The whole time I couldn't move. I often wondered why women who were abused did not just smack their abuser one in the face, and now I knew the answer. My power was completely gone from me.

"No one will respect you," he screamed. "If you stink people will not come near you! You need to open another studio!"

"I have opened four studios, Bikram, and will NOT open another one," I said.

I was in that villa for seven hours. After he had stopped abusing me, the photographs of him came out: him and Elvis, him and Clinton. Then he started talking about his court case and how he had the best lawyer and he was going to win.

In my mind, all I could hear was megalomaniac. He's a megalomaniac. He's a megalomaniac. To be completely honest, I wasn't 100% sure what the true meaning of the word was, but knew it had something to do with power.

When I finally got out of there, I walked back to my room. Jane was walking beside me, very silent and very smug. Something in me wondered whether she was at the bottom of all this behaviour with Bikram, but I could never know. But one thing for sure, she was very smug about the way he had treated me.

I got back to my room, opened the mini bar and drank whisky for the first time in about 10 years. I pretty much drank the mini bar dry. I had to get out of this place. There was no way I wanted to see anyone in the morning. I got online and found another villa around the corner because I couldn't change my flight. I had two more days in Thailand. I was not spending it there with them. I booked the accommodation for the next morning.

The next morning at 6:00 a.m., I got up, showered, dressed, dried my hair, put my makeup on, pulled on a beautiful white dress, put my hair up, put my sunglasses on and walked through the reception looking like Grace Kelly. No one was going to see how broken I was inside.

I hailed a cab and went to my new resort with a private room and pool for the next two days. And that's where I lay out. I'm not quite sure how I managed to get home. It felt like every part of me was in pieces. All I kept thinking of was the devotion that I had shown this man for 10 years and what he'd done to me.

He was like a different person than the person I had met years before. His eyes were even black. Something in me wondered whether he'd been taken over by dark forces.

It felt like Bikram had dumped all of his toxic waste into me. It turned out HE was getting divorced. HE was being accused of rape and had lost the respect of thousands of his students. HE was experiencing people leaving him in droves, changing the name of their studios. HE must have felt like HE stunk. A megalomaniac: the ultimate narcissist. According to Michael Tsarion, a psychic vampire does two things: he draws energy from others, and dumps his own toxic waste into them.

When I arrived home, I spent the next week in the deepest depression I had felt in many years. I just didn't want to be here anymore. I felt like I had nothing left. That's when I went to my doctor and told him I was having negative thoughts and perhaps I was in danger. And he said, "Really? But you look good."

I burst into tears.

"Oh," he said compassionately, as if he just realised I was being serious.

I hid away in my little house with my dogs and went into hibernation. The only time I left the house was to walk the dogs on the beach and to get some supplies.

The next few months consisted of visits to the financial advisor to deal with the debt collectors. Some of them I was able to pay off and some, it was just not possible. These were mostly the electricity bills that had come from the studio.

My Tursa officer, Larry, was a godsend in my life. He was a dark-skinned Englishman with Rastafarian hair and dressed as chic as a rock star, quite opposite to his voice, which was very English and sounded quite dry and straight.

From the beginning, on the first meeting, I liked Larry. He was honest, kind and we developed a nice connection. Sometimes he would say to me, "For God's sake, Norma, can you stop looking like you've just walked out of Windsor Castle?"

All I had done was pull my hair back and put on some lip gloss, the only time I had left the house in a week.

"Well, I'm not looking like a feral," I said, remembering a recent conversation I had had with my mum.

"Dinny let yerself go hen," she said. "No matter what, take care of yerself."

My mum always looked amazing. Even in her 80s she was stylish and immaculately groomed.

"You know, Larry," I said. "Your system really doesn't allow for people like me, people that have been successful and have had their own business and have lost everything. It's fine for people that have never had anything but not for people like me."

He said, "Norma, there IS no one else that comes in here like you."

I said, "No, because you know why? They've all committed suicide."

We both laughed, but we knew that sadly it was true for many poor souls.

One day, I went to see my financial counsellor. I was in a very, very bad place because I had just heard that my mum had been taken into hospital. I really wanted to be with her, but I just didn't have the money to go and visit. It was coming up to Christmas and I just couldn't bear the thought of her being ill and me not being there.

This was one of the few occasions that I had started to cry in that office. Terry had since retired due to a heart condition, and Simone had taken his place. She was also very supportive and lovely and I don't know what I would've done without her.

"You know, Norma," she said, "you really could apply to get some food stamps."

My stomach nearly fell through me.

"Food stamps? No, I could never do that."

She said, "Yes, you can. Come with me."

She took me into an office where I met a lovely girl who took some details and said, "Yes, absolutely. You'd be able to get some help with food. Are you vegan?" she said.

Just a guess, I suppose. She went through to the other room and came back with two bags filled with food. She then told me to go to St Vincent's and I could get some food stamps. There was no way on this earth that I was doing that.

However, I took the bags and walked out to my car. The shame that I felt was beyond belief. Food bags. It reminded me of when I was a little girl at school and my father had left the family. The teacher told me that I would be eligible for discounted meals.

I refused to do that. As I walked back to my car with the food bags, I felt the same shame that 11-year-old girl had. That was the only time that I received help from them. I just couldn't do it again.

Mum got out of the hospital, but she was not well at all. She called me to say that she would like me to go home for Christmas, and she paid for my flight. I had never asked for money from my mum before and it was one of the things I was never good at. However, having been offered her kindness and help, I was definitely willing to take it. I needed to be home, not just for her, but for me as well.

Just before I left to go back to Scotland, my landlord came to visit. He sat down on the step. He looked like he was going to cry.

"Norma," he said. "I am so sorry. This is the hardest thing I've had to do, but I'm going to have to ask you to move out of the house because Paula and I are going to move in. If I don't move into the house soon, I'll never get this other house built." That had been his intention for a long time.

He said, "So it's really hard for me because, to be honest, you're the best tenant I've ever had."

"That's okay, Grant," I replied. "It is just obviously time for me to move on."

Not knowing how on earth I was going to find a place, having no money and two dogs.

CHAPTER FOURTEEN

Final Goodbyes

"Death must be so beautiful. To lie in the soft brown earth, with the grasses waving above one's head, and listen to silence. To have no yesterday, and no to-morrow. To forget time, to forget life, to be at peace."

Oscar Wilde

I arrived in time to be with my mother for Christmas. I was quite shocked to see how thin and frail she was, but she still had her very Scottish wicked sense of humour. I picked out an outfit for Christmas Day, she loved to dress beautifully. I could see that she was quite tired, but happy to have me home. She really had no clue of what I had been going through, nobody did. Except I probably wasn't my jolliest self, as I heard her tell my niece that she thought I was very serious.

One day after Christmas, I decided to go and do a Bikram yoga class in Glasgow and my niece took my mum to the hospital for her check-up. It wasn't looking good and she was kept in that day. The rest of my time in Scotland was visiting my mum daily in the hospital. I was so glad that I was able to be there, but dreading the day that I had to say goodbye. I had to get back for the dogs and also to move house.

The day came to say goodbye and it was a day I'll never forget. When I arrived at the hospital, Mum was already in tears. She was really a strong woman; I hadn't seen her cry many times in my life. She had suffered quite a lot in her lifetime. My father left when I was 11; I saw many tears around that period from her. Her second husband died of a heart condition.

She suffered quite a bit with her health, having been diagnosed with cancer some years prior. Her choice to do radiotherapy really was the worst thing she could have done, because in the words of the surgeon who did her surgery, "I had to remove a metre of your mum's bowel which was dead because of radiotherapy damage. Don't talk to me about radiotherapy, I'm just the one who cleans up the mess it makes."

I was no fan of radiotherapy or chemotherapy; I was a fan of healthy eating and lifestyle. Healthy eating was not the way for somebody in Scotland in their 80s. That generation just wasn't easy to change. The time came for me to leave the hospital and Mum was very emotional; I was very emotional. We hugged each other and I knew it would be the last time I would see her. It was so surreal. I kept looking at her as I walked out and she begged me to go, because she was so upset.

"You'll have to go, my darling, you'll have to go," she sobbed.

I left the hospital and cried the whole way home in the car. The next day, I took the flight from Glasgow back to Brisbane. As the plane took off, the tears started to roll down my face and I could not get them to stop. I had my earphones on, my eyes closed and the tears

Final Goodbyes

were streaming. Someone must've called a flight attendant, because the next thing I felt was a gentle hand on my lap and I heard a voice saying, "What's wrong?" I opened my eyes and said, "I've just said goodbye to my dying mother, I'll never see her again."

The flight attendant was absolutely wonderful. She brought me tissues, she brought me chocolate. Saying things like chocolate fixes everything. I cried the whole way from Glasgow to Dubai. I was still wiping tears away when we landed in Dubai. I honestly thought I was having a complete breakdown, because I was always able to control my emotions, but this time I wasn't. It was like there were just so many tears from all of the things that I had experienced, that they were just not stopping.

When I arrived home, I pretty much fell in a heap of exhaustion. I was in bed for a couple of days, I felt so unwell. I really felt like I needed some help, and it wasn't medicine I needed, it was someone to understand what was happening to my body. I found a healer in the USA that felt right to connect with. Some days this would happen to me, I would be guided to different healers to assist me clear energies I had picked up.

The first thing he said to me was, "What's wrong with your liver?"

"Nothing," I said.

"Do you drink a lot?" he asked.

"No," I replied, "I did when I was younger."

"No, no," he said. "You've got very, very bad liver."

I said, "My mother's cancer has spread to her liver."

"Ah," he said. "Let me check. Oh my goodness, you are tracking your mother. You can't do this, you're going to get really sick. This isn't even yours; 1% of the pain you're feeling in your body, Norma, is yours, the rest is your mother's." And he went on, "You've got so many people in there. How on earth do you walk around?"

"I've been told this so many times," I replied, "but I don't know how to stop it."

He did some energy work on me and it really helped me feel better. Not quite sure how he did it, I never do with these healers, but it helped me. I started to have a little bit more energy.

A few days later my sister called and said that Mum had had a bad experience with a nurse in the hospital and begged my sister to take her home to die. I called my mum and my sister answered the phone, sounding very stressed.

"What's wrong?" I said.

She said, "Mum's medication's been changed and she's really upset."

She put Mum on the phone and I'd never heard my mother like this, she was crying hysterically.

"That's my daughter, that's my daughter on the phone. That's my daughter," she cried to my niece.

My sister came back on the phone and said, "We don't think she's got long."

I jumped out of bed, packed up the majority of the things in my house and decided to go back to Scotland. I found someone to come and stay with the dogs and rent the place while I was gone, that paid for my flight. Amazing what you can do when you have a strong intention. When I arrived back in Scotland, Mum was in bed, out of the hospital. Her wishes were that she would die at home. She did not want to be

Final Goodbyes

in the hospital, especially because the incident with the nurse, who had been very abusive, had made her very scared.

The whole family were in the bedroom, except my older brother. Nieces, nephews, her grandchildren, they were all there. A few days before, I'd been talking to Mum about passing over; she was very scared about dying. I believed, especially because the Nadi leaf reader had told me this, that I would be with my mum at the end, helping her cross over. I believed that part of the reason that I was to be with her at the end was to help her cross over. You see, I've never had any fear of death. I have a strong belief that we do not die, we just change form and leave our bodies behind.

I was able to help my mum understand some of my beliefs and I think it gave her some comfort. At one point, I had gone to the toilet and my niece came out and said, "Aunty Norma, Nana says she's ready to go."

I walked in the bedroom filled with family members and said, "Mum, are you ready to go now?"

"Yes, darling," she said.

"Can I help you?" I said.

"Yes," she replied.

I lay on the bed and held her hand, and as I did, I smelled the most beautiful scent.

I said, "Mum, can you smell the flowers?" She said, "Oh, yes, they're beautiful."

Then I could see all these colours, incredible colours. Not like the colours here, they were quite different, and I said, "Can you see the colours?" And she said, "Oh, they're lovely."

I did not know what was really happening. I was just following some inner guidance. I felt like I was slipping into another dimension and taking Mum there. It seemed I was helping Mum cross over. A friend told me on return I had played the role of a bridgewalker for my dear mum.

Everybody else left; my sister and I stayed with Mum. My sister had one hand; I had the other. I was crying profusely, just asking her to go, because I could feel the suffering. Both of us were whispering in her ear. I was asking Mum just to say, "I want to go back to where I came from, I want to go back to where I came from."

At one point, she started to breathe very uncomfortably; I believe this is called the death rattle. I'd never been with anyone that had died before; my sister had.

My sister looked at me and nodded as if to say she's going. As her last breath left her body, I had never felt the incredible peace I felt at that moment. It was like time stood still. No meditation, no chanting, nothing had ever taken me to that place of peace. It was like my breath stopped and time stopped and there was just an incredible feeling of light. When I looked back at Mum's body, my eyes widened, because I recognised that she was no longer there, it was just a shell of the body that she once inhabited, left in the bed.

The next few days were filled with funeral arrangements and sadness and grief. And a gathering of all the family together for the first time in 30 years. My mum would have loved her funeral as Scottish tradition would have it; we had too many drinks and ended up singing the songs my mum loved to sing. As the time got closer to me leaving Scotland and heading back to whatever lay ahead of me in Australia, the fear of not having money to do what I had to do was looming over my head. One day I went to the local town and sold my wedding ring. Well, I certainly wasn't going to be wearing that ever again. My friends Wendy and Willie dropped me at the airport and said an

Final Goodbyes

emotional goodbye, and I arrived back in Australia with just a few days to leave my house.

I had nowhere to go and very little money. I could not find anywhere that would take two dogs and that I could afford. I even tried caravan parks but could find nothing. I realised during this desperate searching that the anxiety that seemed to be normal for me was reaching levels that had me close to hyperventilating constantly. Two days before I was due to leave the house, I had arranged to put all my furniture in storage and take my dogs and live in my car on the beach. Somehow letting go and accepting this had calmed me down. Less than 24 hours before I packed my dogs into the car, a friend of my dog sitter arrived and we got chatting. She told me about a cottage she had seen for rent on top of a hill. She passed on the number of the owner and I called her. I travelled up the winding road to Wilsons Creek; I had never been up that far before. I met the landlady, then her husband and the next day I moved into the cottage on the hill.

My brother had said to me before I left Scotland, "Norma, don't let the dogs dictate your life."

But the thing is, people didn't really understand that the only reason I had a life was because of my dogs. Because they were the reason that I was here, they gave me purpose. They made me get up every morning and walk them on the beach, which always made me feel better. I had to feed them, I had to take care of them and I wanted to. They were the children that I never had and I loved them more than anything in the world. So, I was happy that I'd found a place where the dogs were welcome. They had lots of land to run around.

I think anyone with depression should go to an animal shelter and rescue a dog or cat. Animals are such healers for our human sorrows. I'm sure they are the real angels here.

I just scraped in enough money to pay the rent and the bond. I found a removalist who did a bit of a budget job and broke a couple of things in the move, but I was very grateful that I was in a new home and not on the beach in my car. It was a one-bedroom cottage, a little bit like a witch's house on top of a hill, which suited me quite fine. It was amazing how I had gone from a six-bedroom house to a one-bedroom cottage, and just got rid of so many things that I didn't need. I realised, living in this small space, that we really don't need much at all.

During this time, I would go down the hill to see my Tursa officer, Larry, to take the dogs to the beach and then I'd be home for the rest of the day alone. It would be days before I would see another human being. It was the most lonely time I had ever experienced in my life, but I certainly didn't have any desire to be with any people either. I felt like I had lost faith in humanity, I felt like I had lost faith in God.

I'd certainly stopped praying around the time my marriage ended, and I had prayed since I was a little girl, up until that point. I seemed to have lost faith in everything. I stopped doing my Kriya yoga, my practice. I stepped away from the people in the ashram and the guru when I became the lady on the hill with the dogs, living in isolation.

During this time, my car went from bad to worse. It had needed quite a few things done, I just didn't have the money to do it. Then I found out it needed a new transmission, which was going to cost about $6,000. So I spent a lot of time not even able to go down to see Larry or to take the dogs to the beach, so I started walking them around the hills. It felt like I was in solitary confinement. Weeks passed and I had not left the cottage except to walk the dogs. Hamish struggled with the steep hills. Even coming up the long, long, steep driveway seemed to be a struggle for him. I noticed that he just wasn't as energetic as he used to be, so I'd walk them as far as he seemed comfortable and then come back to the cottage.

Every week I would select what food I was going to be able to buy once the rent was paid. Sometimes there was no food at all to be bought, so I'd rummage around in my cupboards and see what I could make. I remember thinking, you're not going to break me, whoever I was speaking to in my mind. I found some flaxseeds and an onion and some things to make onion bread and felt a sense of achievement, but many nights I was going to bed hungry.

One day I was looking after my landlord's property whilst they were overseas. I noticed they had a beautiful tree filled with mulberries. So for a week or so, I was taking the mulberries from the tree and eating them or making smoothies. This is how I got through that particular fortnight, food-wise. The dogs always got the last $5 worth of food. Poor Hamish and Bhride—instead of having the lovely food they used to always have, I would have to give them cheap dog food, which just broke my heart, but they didn't mind. In fact, they quite liked it, some of the cheap, nasty stuff. I suppose like we would think about junk food.

Things I had taken for granted I could not buy, such as shampoo, skin creams and sanitary products. I washed my hair with samples that I had collected from my travels. I used aloe vera from my garden to put on my skin and had to use rolled toilet paper when I had my monthly cycle. I still had debt collectors chasing me via email. My phone had been cut off, so I felt relief that they could no longer call me late at night and harass me.

There were many dark nights in that cottage, many sad thoughts and my heart was heavy. Sometimes I would just sit on the daybed and stare off into the view for an hour, sometimes two. I could never, ever have done anything like this, prior to this happening. I spent a lot of time in meditation trying to find out more about me, why I behaved in certain ways, why I tried so hard to please people. Why I had nearly killed myself trying to do the right thing by others, when they were betraying me left, right and centre. Where did this come from, this behaviour?

I recognised that as a child, I had been valued for doing such things. I had the ability to make people feel good, whether it was my smile, my dimples, my laugh, my light, my advice. Whatever it was, I was recognised for helping others. I'm sure this is where this behaviour came from. I decided it was time to change this behaviour and let go of the whole trying-to-save-the-world thing.

I spent a lot of time on the internet researching cancer, especially after my mum, researching all sorts of health and wellness. I did free webinars whenever I could get a chance to and tried to fill my days with educating myself. I thought about all the knowledge that I'd had in this mind of mine. All the years of study in clinical hypnotherapy, aromatherapy, massage, all the books I had read, everything that I had, my yoga, my raw food, and felt like it was all going to waste. Then I decided to put everything that I knew online.

I didn't feel like going and doing classes and teaching people how to eat well, but I could film myself doing it and then that would be able to reach anywhere in the world. Of course, I had no idea how to film, how to edit, how to put videos online, how to make music on the videos. This became my passion for the next year. Within the year, I had five online courses available, from yoga to raw food, to how to ditch dairy, to the Five Tibetan Rites and an e-Book.

I didn't make much money out of them at all, but the process of doing it kept me occupied. I realised it had been such a long time since I had even had a hug. I had never experienced such loneliness. It was like I was changing from someone who used to like being with people, to someone who couldn't stand being with people. The only joy that I got during that time was Hamish and Bhride, my beloved dogs, my angels in fur.

I was contacted by a friend who had a spa in the hills. She asked me to do some massage. I really did not want to but any little bit would help.

Final Goodbyes

I massaged a girl who was a psychologist. As I was massaging her I could feel all this emotion coming out of her solar plexus. "I will not take this on," I promised myself, but knew by the way I was feeling on the drive home that I had.

When I felt overwhelmed with emotion, I craved tobacco. This day was no different. I used to keep a packet of organic tobacco in case of these moments. It just seemed to ground me. I managed to get through the evening by resisting it but by the morning I woke up worse. I had tried to fool myself by putting the tobacco up in the attic, out of reach, so this morning I went outside on the rainy, wet day and brought the ladder inside, propped it up against the attic and climbed up. I grabbed the tobacco and as I went to take the first step down the ladder slipped on the concrete floor and I fell three metres, smashing to the ground. I landed on my head and heard a crack. My arm was twisted behind my back in between the ladder and my back. I think I was out for a bit and when I opened my eyes I asked myself, "Am I still alive?" The tears poured down my face as I screamed out in agony and I tried to free my arm from the weight of the ladder. I got myself free, rolled a cigarette with one hand and smoked it. My hand was throbbing, my head was pounding and I was shaking all over. I got in the car and started driving down the hill. My neighbour stopped me and asked where I was going. She said, "Norma, you are as white as a ghost, you are in shock. I'll drive you."

She took me to the hospital where I was scanned, poked, prodded, X-rayed and had my arm put in a cast. I was told I was very lucky that I had not received any major damage.

My ribs were badly bruised and the pain was incredible. It was a few days before Christmas; I caught a cold and every sneeze was agony. I could not drive and sat in the cottage in such despair that I could not see a way out. I wrote out a will of sorts, so that if anything happened to me, there were instructions for what I wanted for Hamish and Bhride. I was finally done.

CHAPTER FIFTEEN

My Angels

"For I am with you, and no one will attack you to harm you, for I have many in this city who are my people."
Acts 18:10

Hamish's energy seemed to be getting worse, so I called in the vet. As soon as he saw him, he said, "Norma, stop giving him the tick medicine."

"Why?" I said, "You told me to give it to him when we moved up here to the hills."

"Yes, I know," he said. "But I've seen another dog suffer and I think it's got something to do with a tick medicine, so just take him off it and see how he goes."

I did, but the energy never really came back for Hamish. Alan had been the vet for the dogs for many years and I trusted him but sadly he was retiring due to his own health concerns.

One day I was grooming Hamish and I noticed a little lump under his neck. It was quite tiny, but I decided to have it checked anyway. I took him to a nearby vet and they did a biopsy. Within 24 hours of having the biopsy, the tiny lump was the size of a huge red plum. It wasn't very long before they gave me the results of that, a day or two, I remember, but I nearly fell over when the vet told me that Hamish had cancer.

It was only a year since my mum had passed. Having suffered the same horrible condition and treatment for it, I was so confused as to what to do, but I certainly didn't want to get him cut open and given poison chemotherapy or radiotherapy, which had in my mind been the reason that my mother's life had ended.

"He needs to have surgery," said the vet, "and he needs to then go on chemotherapy." The vet assured me that was the only thing that would have helped him.

I hung up the phone and lay down on the carpet. The dogs knew something was wrong because they came either side of me and sandwiched me. I started to howl, hugging Hamish, as Bhride squeezed into me, comforting me. I cried and cried and then I heard myself say, "Please don't take my dog. Please don't take my dog. You've taken everything else. Please don't take my dog."

And then an anger started to boil within me as my words changed to, "You're not taking my fucking dog. You've had everything else."

This anger was enough to give me some energy to stand up. I was pacing around the cottage like a panther, wondering what I could do to stop this from happening.

My Angels

I got online and started researching dogs with cancer and the type of tumour that he had, which was a mass cell tumour. I contacted someone in Melbourne who had a business making healthy dog products and he suggested to have a hair analysis, which is exactly what I did. I cut a little bit of Hamish's hair off and sent it away for analysis. What came back a week later was that Hamish had poison in his liver, kidneys and pancreas and colon. I was pretty sure this was the poison from the tick medicine. The strange thing was that Bhride had had the same tick medicine, but Bhride was a very different beast to Hamish. I was told by a dog trainer that Bhride was an alpha female, so she seemed to have a lot stronger immune system and in general was a stronger dog than Hamish. What would I do if I had chemicals in my system?

I would detox. Hamish went on a detox with bone broth and psyllium to clear his colon. The naturopath who did the hair analysis sent some herbs to assist with this. I also used aloe arborescence, which was a treatment some people had used for cancer. And I heard people were getting great results with medical cannabis with cancer, so that was my next topic of research. The vet was adamant that I needed to book in to have the surgery, so I did it, telling her that I would have some time to think about it over the week. I found someone who supplied medical cannabis, who was well known in the local area.

This person was so willing to help me that he met me at 9:00 p.m. in the town. I felt like I was doing something really bad, meeting someone and getting some cannabis, which was illegal, and then giving it to my dog.

I had a trip to Noosa booked with the dogs. I considered cancelling it due to Hamish's condition but decided to go. That would be my week of pondering what to do with regards to the surgery. The surgery was booked for the following Monday. During my stay in the Noosa, it was pretty much filled with me researching cannabis, cancer, dog's cancer, researching all types of nutrition for dogs with cancer and it was so confusing. I wanted to pull my hair out, everybody was saying different things. They need to have a lot more meat, they need to have no meat, they need to have less, more fat and less carbs.

It was a lot like the human diet dilemma. Everybody was confused about the right things to eat. I continued to give Hamish his CBD and his aloe vera and by the time we got back home his tumour had reduced back down slightly and become dry like a scab healing. I thought perhaps that this would continue. The type of tumour was one that bled quite easily and before long the tumour was bleeding regularly.

I decided to get bandages and take care of the tumour because my understanding was the problem was internal and even if the tumour was taken off, the condition was still there within him. Although I had to see the tumour bleeding and all of this stuff coming out, he seemed to have more energy. It was like all of the bad stuff was coming out through the tumour. I cancelled the surgery and found a holistic vet in Noosa who gave me a very thorough phone consultation and helped me understand the best things I could do. He sent me herbs to give him internally and herbs to put on the tumour. Meanwhile, I was still researching, trying different diets. I consulted with a nutritionist especially for dogs in the UK who told me exactly what to do. I made my first trip to the organic butcher in many years as I hadn't eaten meat for so long.

One day at the markets I bumped into a friend I hadn't seen for a long time. Kate and I got chatting about what we had been up to over the last period of time and when I told her about my situation, she shook her head and said, "Norma, have you ever thought that you might have a curse on you?"

As crazy as it sounds, I said, "Yes, Kate, I have. I don't understand why all these bad things have happened to me."

My Angels

"It does happen, you know," she said. "It's just not normal to have all these bad things happening, one after the other."

Her words stayed with me. Mum had left me some money and it had finally come through so I was in a position to get some help. One day whilst I was browsing through the internet, I listened to someone called Chris being interviewed on YouTube, on a channel I listened to quite often. He called himself a holographic healer. I straight away knew I had to get in touch with this person. He was in Canada. Thankfully his fees were very low. He seemed to be a decent, all-round nice guy, but had some ability to clear energy from people. I really was beginning to think that something dark had entered my life. When I finally got the appointment with Chris, it was all confirmed.

The first thing he said to me was, "My dear, you've had a suicide curse put on you."

Chris was not an airy-fairy type of healer. He was a down-to-earth guy who didn't have feathers hanging around him or wishy-washy talk. He was a very normal type of guy that obviously had a gift. He used the sacred geometry to start and clear those curses from me and some other dark entities and energies that he could see. As he was doing clearing, I actually felt something being lifted from me.

When he used his neutraliser ring to clear me, I felt my whole body start to sway. It was incredible the lightness that I felt after the session with him. Within 24 hours, I felt glimpses of the old Norma coming through.

Then he said to me, "Norma, it's no wonder you get so attacked. You have such a huge amount of—" (something I could not pronounce).

And I said, "What is that? What does that mean?"

He said, "You have so much biphotonic light in you that you would be like the crème de la crème of food for these dark entities; they're feeding off you. They're feeding off your life-force. Keeping you in a low vibrational state, in suffering and depression. That is their food source. They can't feed off love, which is our natural state."

A few years ago I would have thought this man was absolutely insane , but I knew what he was saying was true. I felt drained. I couldn't understand why all of this change had happened in my life in such a negative way and I couldn't seem to get myself out of it. I thought I was strong but had felt like a victim with all of these punches keeping me down. I knew that there were vampire-type entities feeding off people on this planet. I knew about a lot of things that I didn't always share with people; I had done quite a bit of research into them. It's not the kind of thing that you would say to many people, that you believe that this planet's been taken over by dark forces and with a vampiric type of energy feeding on the light of those of us connected to Source. I had learned that even our relationships can be interfered with so that we are 'set up' with partners who trigger us. Being triggered, and feeling deep pain and sadness from our core wounds, can be food for the interdimensional beings.

After my session with Chris, I really felt so much better; between that and the medical cannabis that I was also now taking, I really started to feel like there was hope coming at the end of the tunnel. A few months later I came across another healer that I was listening to who also stood out for me. I knew that I also had to connect with this person. She was also from Canada.

This woman had also been through incredibly challenging times with attacks and being targeted by dark forces. The small session with her turned into a three-hour session. I told her that by this time I had stepped away from the ashram and from doing all of the Kriya yoga, chanting and processes that I had been doing when I was part of the ashram in India and following the guru.

She told me that most of my suffering had come from me giving my power away to the gurus and other types of beings. It didn't come as a surprise because I had already started to pick up that this might be the case. Although I didn't think it was all of the reasons. I do believe that something was going on in the ashram where I was being drained of energy. Before the session with her I had given up reading any of these scripture-type books. I had given up the meditations, the chanting, the prayers and everything that I had done previously that was connected to the ashram. I had removed all the photos of the guru and even disconnected from all the friends I had made in the ashram.

She said to me, "Norma, people only take our energy when we give them permission. They really don't have the strength or the ability to take energy from us unless we have given permission. You've got some work to do. You need to go through every single ceremony, every chant, every prayer, every ashram visit that you have done, and you need to revoke all of those contracts because what you've done is entered into contracts with these beings. That's the only way they can take your energy."

After my session with Lauda, I spent hours trying to remember all of the ceremonies that I had taken part in in India and Byron Bay and all the other places. Where I had chanted words that I didn't even know the meaning of. I know now that chanting these type of words can invoke entities from other dimensions.

I had about four A4 pages written of ceremonies that I had done over the years. I did a very clear revocation prayer and revoked every contract that I had entered into consciously or unconsciously, so that these contracts were declared null and void. One of the things that Lauda had said to me on the Skype session was, "Norma, your life has been hijacked. You have a whole team of beings working against you, trying to keep you down, trying to stop you doing what you came to this planet to do."

"That's exactly how I feel. I feel like I'm a mushroom with somebody standing over the top of me so that I can't grow."

"You're much more powerful than any of them and you can stop it," she said, "once you clear all the contracts."

It reminded me of the time I had made the onion bread. I said loudly, "You're not going to bring me down," speaking to whoever was keeping me locked down, because that's exactly how it felt.

"You're not going to break me. You are not going to stop me." And then I said, "Gee, I must be here to do something important if you're putting so much energy into stopping me, you bastards!"

The sessions with Lauda and Chris really helped me get clear on what had been happening to me. I knew I was an empath. I knew by this time that I carried a lot of light. There was a saying I learned in India: "The amount of light that you carry will be met with the same amount of darkness trying to stop it." I was aware that there were noticeable changes in the people around me—my students, my partners, my friends—because in this light it will always bring up other people's darkness. It wasn't always pleasant. People weren't always able to be around me for long periods of time, but I knew that when people spent time with me, there were changes within them.

Somebody described me once as a catalyst for change in people. I was beginning to understand that this now. It didn't make me better than anyone else or higher than anyone else or any of that ego stuff. But going back to what Nicole told me was that I came here as a volunteer; having done the work, I rested my spiritual growth so that I could come and help others. My mission, I was beginning to remember, was to path cut, to be a way shower, to go ahead of other people, find a way through the challenging times, and then leave that energetic path open for them. So that when they went through it, it wouldn't be quite as challenging.

My Angels

The relief I felt, and starting to know a little bit more about who I was and why I was here, was so empowering for me. One of the gifts in being an empath is that when you know the truth, you feel it in your body and when you hear a lie, you also feel the schism in your body. I wish I had felt this before, but I was only just beginning to experience it. This was a truth that I was hearing. So not only did I discover that I was here as an undercover angel, volunteer, helper, path cutter, way shower, but I was being helped by other angels, way showers, path cutters and healers to remind me of who I was.

Lauda, Chris, Nicole and many, many more were brought into my path so that they could remind me of why I came and what I was here to do. It all started to make sense as to why these things were happening to me, why I felt like I was being attacked on all levels. But I also knew now that stepping into my power, nothing had power over me and would never have power over me again.

During the time I was taking care of Hamish I became so interested in the medical cannabis that I started studying it. I did a certificate course online to learn about all the aspects of medical cannabis. I was so impressed with the way that I was feeling. I'm sure it was helping me get through the trauma of Hamish's illness.

One day I went in to get some more cannabis from my supplier, then asked him out of the blue if he would like some help.

"I'd love to have someone like you help me," Samuel said, "because you've got a health background. I really want this to be a clinic to be a healing place where people come to get help."

I suggested that I do consultations on health and diet and also having an understanding, now on cannabis, I could help the clients understand how it all works. I didn't know how energetic I was after my illness, if I would be able to work, but I thought I'd give it a go.

I started to support Samuel's clinic one half day a week and then two half days. I was starting to feel better. It was nice to be with people again. I'm sure by this time I was aware that it was actually ingrained into my soul to help others.

I now felt confident enough to ask for a consultation fee and was able to step away from Centrelink, which was the most wonderful feeling. I also decided it was necessary for me to learn more about the correct diet for these clients. Many of them had cancer, chronic disease such as fibromyalgia, arthritis. Many, many people had depression and anxiety and many people were very confused about what to eat. As a raw food chef I knew what was good for me to eat, but what of those with cancer? I had gone through my own confusing times with Mum and so I decided to study with someone who was getting results.

In my research I came across Dr Robert Morse. He was a naturopathic doctor and a biochemist. I loved listening to him. He had YouTube videos about many different types of conditions and was getting incredible results. I decided he was the one I wanted to study under and of course I wasn't able to, at this stage, to do his course and fly to America. I was able to do the home study course. I learned so much from Dr Morse. I learned about the simplicity of the diet that was necessary for the body to get well, going back to nature, fruits, berries, melons and vegetables. Raw, living foods was the easiest diet, but when I did talk to people about it, they would say, "Well, what would I eat?"

It was interesting because that was really the type of food that I was eating when I was well. When I wasn't well, it was another story. I knew the power of fruits and berries and melons and vegetables because I ate mostly that myself. Of course, I did eat a lot of raw food as well, making my own biscuits, crackers and breads when I was on top of it financially, and that was about to change as well because my mum's house that she had left to us had been sold.

My Angels

That was a strange feeling, knowing that my family home was gone. The relief was that my mum had left us all some money and before long this money came through and got me out of the darkest times I had ever been in. I was able to buy a new little car and sell the troublesome Jeep that had cost me so much money for a fraction of what I had paid for it. I was able to have food in my fridge again and buy what I wanted at the fresh food markets. It was such a great feeling to have some money in the bank again. Things really were shifting.

After six months, I completed my certificate with Dr Morse as a Detoxification Specialist. This was an incredible addition to the consultations that I was doing in medical cannabis. I still continued to study medical cannabis and even did a few more certificates. My evenings were spent listening to some of the professors who had a wealth of knowledge in medical cannabis and Dr Morse videos. I could not get enough information, because when I was sitting with these clients who had been told that they were going to die, they needed someone to listen, someone who could advise them about medical cannabis and what to eat. Changing their diets certainly was a big part of it. Many of the people that were told that they only had so long to live are still here today. People don't understand how important the diet is. It's really number one.

Before long, I was getting referrals from doctors, even oncologists, and many of the clients I had seen and given advice to were sending their friends and their loved ones to see me. I only ever worked half days. I really didn't want to go back to having any form of chronic fatigue. I never worked weekends. Even if people begged me to come and see them, to help them, I'd never work weekends. I had to take care of myself. This is something that I learned. In order to help other people, you have to take care of yourself first. This is something that made a huge difference to me.

One of the lessons that came out of those challenges that I went through was you can only give from a full cup. You can't give from an empty cup, and I was putting this into action very well. Sometimes I would come home after seeing two clients and rest for the rest of the day, but I knew when to say no. This was also helping me buy Hamish's medical cannabis, which was so important for me. It was almost like it was only because of Hamish that I was doing this. It was my love for him that encouraged me to do it and he was my priority over everything.

CHAPTER SIXTEEN

Promise to a Dog

"Dogs have a way of finding the people who need them, and filling an emptiness we didn't ever know we had."
                                                  Thom Jones

Hamish was always his most beautiful, loving self. No matter what. He never seemed to show any suffering. He never seemed to be in pain. I always worried that he was; I would sit there on the floor with him and clean his tumour and then put whatever the vet had given me to put on it. There were certain herbs for that type of tumour. I sometimes put cannabis oil on it and he would sit there gently looking at me lovingly as I took care of it.

One night as I was cleaning his tumour and wrapping his bandage round, the tears were streaming down my face. Hamish was a very respectful dog. He never walked in a door before me. He never licked at my face, but this time he did. He gently started licking the tears and licked every part of my face, and when I opened my eyes he was looking in my eyes with such love and comfort as if to say, "It's okay, Mum, I'm okay."

It got to the stage I was changing his bandages three or four times a day. This tumour was bleeding so much. I contacted my vet in Noosa and asked him what to do.

"If we remove the tumour, will it come back?" I asked him.

He said, "There's a 50-50 chance, but it sounds like it's not getting better, Norma."

I packed the dogs in the car and drove four hours north to Noosa. The vet was amazing. Hamish had the surgery; I was there with him when he woke up. He was given a vitamin C infusion to assist with clearing out the residue from the anaesthetic. I then drove all the way back home. The next day we all sat on the couch for most of the day, tired. I was so exhausted. By the time the bandages were removed, Hamish was jumping around the beach like a puppy. It was such a wonderful scene, but before long the tumour started to grow back, this time under the skin, so there was no exit for the poisons and the toxins unfortunately. I could see that his energy was fading and he was losing weight. I knew that I was going to lose my boy.

One day I was having a consultation with a lady on the phone and she told me she had worked in the vets for many years and that she had the ability to communicate with animals.

She told me that for 20 years she had helped the vets and the one thing she was aware of was that dogs did not want help when they were ready to go. It was an interesting topic because I was battling with what to do when the time came for Hamish. I asked her if she could help me find a little bit more about what Hamish wanted. She was only too willing to help. She went into a quiet space, asked me his name, and then told me that he had done what he came here to do. Of course, I started to cry because I knew that one of the things Hamish came here to do was help me survive those challenging times. It seemed to be that now I was on a new path, I was helping others again, I was doing something that made me feel good, perhaps he was ready to go now and leave me this new legacy.

"He doesn't want help," she said. "Let him go naturally."

I had received the number of a lady who helped pets pass on and had her number sitting beside my computer. I looked at it and thought, I'll never call you, but as the time got closer and Hamish's energy was weaker, I was so scared that he was suffering. How could I know? He was always looking at me lovingly. I called the lady to ask her what she did and she told me she was lovely, very kind, compassionate, and I said to her, "I hope I never have to call you, but thank you for your information."

When Hamish finally lost interest in food, I knew the end was near. Hamish, a golden retriever who lived for food, turning his nose up at food was definitely not a good time. I had received some herbs for him a week or so before from a local lady who also had the ability to communicate with animals.

She was named the horse whisperer. She works with a lot of horses. She was quite lovely, and I told her of my dilemma of what to do when the time comes. She also did a little check-in and she said, "No, he doesn't really want help, but, Norma, that may change because just like humans, we change our mind. They can change their mind too."

One morning Hamish just would not get off the bed. He used to jump down, have his breakfast and then get excited about going to the beach. I knew this day was different. I decided to wash the bedroom windows and just be around the bedroom with him. All day he lay on the bed. At times, I would sit with him, cuddle him, rock him, talk to him. One of the things I had told him was that it was okay for him to go.

I said, "You know, you have to go. I want you to go naturally if that's what you want, so please go and I'm going to be okay."

I was crying and he could also feel that, I'm sure. He finally got off the bed with a little bit of help from me, went to the toilet and then spent the rest of the afternoon on the floor. I lay down beside him and said, "Hamish, you're obviously suffering. I want you to go. You've been an awesome friend and I love you more than anything in the world. And I promise I'll move out from the cottage on the hill. I'll move back to be with people again and who knows, I may even find a boyfriend. I promise you, Hamish, I'll be okay and I've got Bhride Baggins to take care of me, so please know that I'm going to be okay and maybe come back at the end of my life so that we can have another few years together and we'll go home together."

This was my promise to my dog.

I tucked him up on top of the bed and could not sleep. I called the lovely lady who was the one who helped the pets say goodbye and told her he was near the end. She offered to come then and I said, "No, I want them to go through the night and see how he goes." It was a long night. I was rocking him or stroking him. He had some painkillers, but I wasn't to know if he was in pain. Bhride seemed to sense what was going on and decided to sleep in the lounge room that night.

At seven o'clock in the morning, he was still there and I could tell he wasn't good. There was no coming back from where he was now. I called the lady who said she would come straight away. I had a conversation with God; well, more like a screaming match, screaming monologue with God. I said, "How could you do this? How could you let something so beautiful suffer? He has been everything to me." I walked around the bedroom screaming, crying, wiping tears, kissing him and I felt like I was going insane.

This was to be a decision that I had to make. It really went against my beliefs, but it was what I had to do in my mind to help him pass. When she arrived, she said, "We have to be quick."

"Why? I said. "Maybe he'll just go naturally."

"Norma, his heart is so strong," she replied, "he could stay like this for days. They don't tend to go naturally."

She explained the procedure about putting in the relaxant and then their final injection. As soon as she told me I was so traumatised, I went to the toilet and had diarrhoea.

"Can we just put the relaxant in and see if he goes?" I said. Which she was happy to do. She put the relaxant in.

His eyes were already distant even before she arrived. When she snapped her fingers around his eyes, he didn't respond at all. That's why I really hoped that he would go on his own. During that 20 minutes after the relaxant, I was begging him, "Hamish, please, go, please, go, please, go so we don't have to give you this injection."

But she said after the 20 minutes his heart was just as strong. I believe his heart was so strong for me, and then she said, "We have to do it now."

It was the most horrible thing that I've ever had to do. Then she turned to me and said, "That's it."

"That's it?" I said. "He's gone?" It was so quick and nothing like what it was to watch my mother pass. There was no sense of peace here. The only peace that eventually came was knowing that he wasn't suffering.

I left the room, and went into the lounge room where Bhride was waiting for me. I was in so much shock. I just couldn't believe that he was gone. This was nothing like watching my mother pass. It was so much more painful. The vet wrapped him in a beautiful white sheet and asked where I wanted him to lay until the undertaker came, so we put him on his favourite part of the lounge. This part of the lounge that was covered in scratches because of his nails. He always sat there and cuddled right into my legs.

She sprinkled petals around him and asked if he had a favourite toy. Hamish loved toys, but he seemed to like the green ones more than any other colour, so we put a little green crocodile next to him. He lay there, looking like he was sleeping. The vet was incredible. She was so compassionate. She stayed with me for another half an hour or so. She organised the undertaker to come. She was quite incredible. Nothing like it would have been if I had gone to a vet, no sterile environment, and I'm sure this was the way Hamish would have liked it too, to be at home on his favourite bed and then his lounge with Mum. I sat beside him, staring at the clock, dreading the moment the undertaker came. When he did he also was incredibly compassionate and advised me not to make any decisions about what I wanted to do with his remains right now, to have a think about it over the week.

He took Hamish's little frail body, which used to be 37 kilos and was now about 27, out to the van and put him on a little tray. One of the extremely difficult things in that procedure was watching Bhride follow Hamish out to the van. She sat there and watched his little body get put into the van as if to go, "Come on, come and play. Come and play with a ball."

It was so heartbreaking. The undertaker asked if I wanted to come and say goodbye. At this point, my neighbour had arrived because she had seen the van arrive and she stood there giving me some lovely support, which was really welcomed. I kissed his little head goodbye and said, "I'll see you when you come back. Now, go and have a well-deserved rest, my angel, I'm going to be okay, remember my promise."

Promise to a Dog

Everybody left and I was there alone with Bhride, not quite knowing what to do. One of the things that I did like to do when I felt extremely emotional was have a bath; in this little cottage there wasn't a bath, but I did have a secret swimming hole that I used to go to in the upper part of the mountains, so I grabbed Bhride, got in the car and said, "Come on." I used to take Hamish and Bhride there regularly in between the beach visits. I was still in disbelief when I arrived at the swimming hole. I sat on the edge on a rock because Bhride swam in the water and played with sticks and sniffed around. I stripped off, got in the water and went completely under. When I came up, I was howling; the tears were pouring down my face.

Each time I dipped in the water, I would come up feeling a little bit more cleansed and then I heard my inner voice say, "Well, Norma, what story are you going to give yourself about this one? Are you going to play victim? Talk about how terrible it was, how painful it was, how sad it is, or are you going to take the other path? And acknowledge that Hamish had an incredible life and he was deeply, deeply loved and that it was just his time to go and he only left because he knows that you're safe. Which story are you going to tell yourself, Norma?"

I knew immediately which story I was going to tell myself. The latter, and I would stick with that. I dipped under the water again and jumped up. The water was cold and refreshing against my skin and the tears stopped. We stayed there for a little bit longer. Something had changed. Something was much calmer in me and very accepting of everything I had just witnessed. I was still quite perplexed as to how calm I was.

"Come on, Bhride," I said. "Hamish has gone to sleep. You're the top dog now."

When I got home to the cottage, I wrote this little poem to help release a bit. I often wrote poems when I was hurting.

Undercover Angel

For Hamish, a Living Angel

There are no words than can express the love I have for you,

I said 100 times or more each day "my Golden Boy, I love you"

And then a few more 100 times as the end of the day drew near

And then before we went to bed I whispered in your ear, that I love you more than the whole big world cos you're the best boy here

Today I had to make the call, that no one wants to make,

And wondered when the vet arrived if it was a big mistake,

I hoped you'd go whilst deep asleep

And prayed each night you might

I did not want to be the one you see, to take away your life

And when she put the needle in I asked her just to wait …

I was still not ready to let you go, and feared my heart would break

And break it did completely, when I looked into your eyes

I know you would not have left, you see, you could not say goodbye

So I had to do the hardest thing and watch you slip away

The pain so bad within me, would I survive this awful day?

Promise to a Dog

I sat beside your body surrounded with sweet flowers

And kept looking at the clock because they were coming in an hour

I cried so much, I'm so, so deeply sorry, my angel, my beautiful Golden Boy

But you could no longer lick my tears, you were asleep beside your favourite toy

I watched your little body get put into the van and Bhride standing at the door beside the undertaker man

Your body was so little now, that cancer is so mean

I thought I would forget to breathe, the pain was so extreme

It took away my soulmate, my forever bestest friend

So broken is my heart to see this coming to an end …

Your name was always on my lips as people rolled their eyes

At the crazy dog lady in the hills who loved animals more than guys

My Hamish was my one true love who has my heart for life

I hope one day it will not feel as it does right now

Stabbed deeply with a knife …

CHAPTER SEVENTEEN

Return to Love and Purpose

"There will come a time when you believe everything is finished; that will be the beginning."

Louis L'Amour

After Hamish had passed, I knew that I had to move out of the cottage, as I promised him. It felt so different without him. I started to look around, but it was very difficult, in the area that I wanted to be, having a dog. So many people would just have no dogs, no animals!!! No dogs!!! No pets!!! Without even meeting you.

One day I got a call from a client. It was a Saturday morning. She asked me if I had any medicine as she was going through a very difficult time of withdrawal. I didn't have any medicine, but I did have some leftover medicine that was Hamish's. I could hear the desperation in her voice, so broke my rule about not working on the weekend and went to meet her to take her the medicine. I met her in the car park. I gave her the medicine and she asked me what I was doing. I told her I was looking for a new place to live, but I was finding it difficult having a dog. She mumbled something about having to one day find someone to move in with her as she had recently separated from her husband. The rest of the day was a bit of a disappointment as nothing was showing up in regards to a positive outcome.

That afternoon, I got a text from the lady I had met that morning. She sent me a picture of her house and asked me to have a look at it. She said that up until now, she had never met anyone that she thought she could share with, but she thought she could share with me. I opened up the link and looked at the most magnificent house—a huge house with a whole lower floor with three bedrooms, beautiful wardrobes, including an office as well as upstairs where she lived. She offered me the whole of the lower floor for a very low rent. I couldn't believe my eyes. It was so beautiful and it was on an acre of land that was fully fenced with an electric gate so that Bhride would be safe. She finished the text by saying, "God cares."

The next day I went to see the house and it was even better in reality. That was to become our new home. I absolutely loved it. It was around the corner from the clinic. Bhride was still suffering from losing her big brother and best friend, and having a huge, safe, grassy area to run around in and someone there when I was with clients was such a blessing.

Sharon and I became good friends very quickly. While we still had our own space, she lived upstairs, I lived downstairs. She was a born-again Christian and sometimes her conversations would go well into our different beliefs but we were able to live with each other in harmony.

"I think you're going to meet someone," Sharon said about a week after I moved in.

She was right. One day I got a Facebook message from a friend that I had hardly heard from in the last 12 years. She said, "Call me, call me."

I got her number and called her and said, "What's wrong?"

"I have a boy for you!" she excitingly shrieked. "I can't believe I haven't thought of it before. He lives there. You live there. He's got a business background. You've got a business background. I think you guys would be awesome together. Can I give him your number?"

"Well, you know what, Elissa?" I said. "Perfect timing; I made a promise I am going to keep and I'm going to date a lot of men. So, sure, you can give him my number."

A few days later I received a text from Mark. I had looked at his Facebook profile my friend Elissa had given me and he looked like a normal, good-looking guy. Mark texted me and we organised to meet in a local café. When I met him in the flesh, he was even nicer. He was very handsome to me: well dressed, had slicked grey hair, a wicked smile and was hysterically funny. We laughed our heads off. I think I talked more during that coffee meeting than I had in months. I had been on my own for so long. It was so nice to talk to someone and have fun. At the end of our meeting, he took my hand and said, "I think we should have dinner."

"I think we should too," I replied with a smile.

Mark had also gone through his fair share of relationships, suffering and pain. I wondered what it would be like dating someone again after so long. I had been single for five and a half years with only a small two-week relationship in the middle of that, which I was no way near ready for. I wondered whether I would be able to trust again. I remember whilst I was in the hills writing a list of what I really wanted in a man. It consisted of components of all my other relationships. I thought if I could just meet someone that had all of these different aspects, that would be the perfect man for me. I had written that list and I remember finding it as I was packing up to leave the cottage on the hill. I read it again and ripped it up and said out loud, "I'm not good at picking men. You can pick one for me, God".

Maybe he did because Mark seemed to have every single quality on that list.

We took our relationship very slowly. My intention of dating lots of men didn't happen. I was very happy spending time with Mark. He introduced me to the members of his family, who were adorable. His mother and father were absolutely charming. They were retired ministers of the church and were very loving to me. Mark used to joke that they loved me more than they loved him. It was so lovely to be able to go out again with someone. I'd forgotten how it felt to go out for dinner or the movies or just to hang out on the weekend at his house. He even got me to sing again. I loved to sing and had not done it for years. We were a cute little duo—Mark played the guitar and piano and I sang.

It wasn't like any other relationship I had had in the beginning. Mostly in the beginning of my relationships it had happened very fast. This one was slow and gentle and we both knew that we had things to work through, we had both experienced a lot of hurt and at one point we decided very clearly that we would try to work through any issues that arose as a couple. We made a commitment that we wanted to be with each other and knew that some of our wounds from the past could arise. If they did we made a commitment to go through them together and support each other.

The first year of that relationship I was triggered so many times. My fear of being hurt again was enormous. Would I ever trust again? I was told in a meditation that Mark was the one who would help me heal this wound and I would assist him trusting and loving again. It was not easy to face these fears. Multiple times I wanted to run away. It was so much easier to be alone as I had been for so long, but I knew the only way to heal was to face the pain and I was over doing life alone.

When wounds surfaced, we just got through them. I learned to not react but to go within, feel my pain and talk with Mark afterward, and Mark learned to not withdraw. With a background in psychology, he was able to hear me but did not always understand me—not many people could. He was very much an intellectual and worked things out in his head. I was a deep feeler as an empath and even felt a lot of the pain he was carrying but was not aware of. I felt so much of what he had buried within him and had soldiered on with.

This was the most adult relationship I had ever been in. Another thing that seemed different about our relationship was that we didn't seem to need each other. This was interesting and again, quite different for me. We seemed to be in a place where each of us individually was happy in our own skin and where we were happy together. For me, I think this came from the amount of time I spent alone. I think during that time one of the positive things that came out of it was that I learned to like my own company. I really didn't seem to need anyone, which meant that choosing to spend time with Mark was very different than needing someone in my life. I'm sure this gave him freedom that he hadn't experienced before. It really made me see how much I had changed during that time alone. I loved spending time with Mark, but I also enjoyed spending time by myself. It seemed to be that that was necessary for me now.

I was told in my meditations that I would learn more about energy in this relationship. Sometimes I would feel an emotion and just know it was not mine, it was Mark's. Instead of taking it on, I would lovingly send it back. Sometimes I would feel aches in my body that Mark had. I even felt hungover if he had more than a few drinks. All of it teaching me to take more care of myself and know what was mine and what was not.

Within a year, I had moved to a gorgeous little apartment on the beach, one of my favourite beaches. It was the same beach I walked Bhride at most days, so I felt very blessed to find the most adorable little apartment with a garden, where I walked out my gate, across the path and onto the beach. It felt like heaven. Things were really changing in my life. I had always wanted to live on the beach. It seemed to be that the darkness was leaving me. I felt happy again. I felt fulfilled in my relationship. I felt fulfilled in what I was doing career-wise, learning more and more about medical cannabis and diet and health and helping others. I loved my time alone. I loved my time with Mark. I loved my time with my clients. Some weekends we would spend at my house on the beach and other weekends we would spend at Mark's house in the country. It was a beautiful balance. We would decide during the week whether we wanted a country weekend by the pool at Mark's house or a beach weekend by the ocean at mine. We visited Scotland and had a wonderful time together. There was so much laughter between us. My family adored him and he fitted in so well. We visited Plockton and met my second cousin who was now running the Plockton Hotel. There was a ceilidh on the night we stayed and the sound of Scottish music and people singing filled the hotel. Mark loved the breathtaking scenery as much as I did. We visited whisky distilleries and I found a new love for my own country's single malts. We caught up with friends along the road trip and Mark learned a lot more about my childhood and culture. The struggle again for us was the food; it was a challenge finding a good salad anywhere, but the whisky and people made up for it. We required a 10-day juice fast on return to try to get back to normal. It also took me a trip to Bali for a complete cleanse with colonics, yoga and body scrubs to finally feel like my old self again.

Mark retired in January 2020 and we decided to kick off his new beginning with some rest and relaxation on a trip to Bali. The two weeks would be broken up into an indulgent week on Gili Air, which we just loved every minute of, followed by a week in the resort in Ubud where I had run my wellness retreats from. That week consisted of a three-day juice fast followed by a four-day raw food journey. With Bikram yoga to sweat out the toxins and body scrubs and seaweed wraps we came home glowing. Mark was so open to trying all my weird and wonderful health tips because he believed in me and regularly told me he was my biggest fan and was very proud of what I did.

"My Scottish warrior princess," he would call me when he heard me swearing at some injustice to animals or news about corrupt governments. After two years we decided to move in together and rented a beautiful house near the beach. Mark adored Bhride and she him and we became a wonderful little family. Slow and steady we nurtured ourselves and each other and witnessed our union grow into a beautiful, loving relationship.

Being fulfilled with what I was doing was crucial to my happiness too. I was more and more impressed with what this amazing plant, cannabis, could do. The stories that my clients were telling me about how their lives had changed, people with suicidal depression being happy again, people with arthritis relieved of pain, people with fibromyalgia, Lyme disease, autism, little children feeling better and having more interaction with their family. The changes I was seeing in people were incredible. Some of the most regular clients to visit my clinic were cancer patients. Some of them would come in having been told that they would only have so long to live. The first thing I would do was encourage them not to lose hope. I would explain many different types of healing available that have had success. I had witnessed people who had been given the death sentence and were still here two years later. Sometimes giving them hope was really the best thing I could do, because by having hope, at least they would be in a better frame of mind for whatever happened. It was very confronting for me having people choose to do chemotherapy and radiotherapy because it would never be my choice, especially after watching my mum suffer with what radiotherapy did to her.

Sometimes I would send my clients things to listen to, videos of doctors who had great results with their patients using natural products. Sometimes I would send them information to read and educate themselves and sometimes I wouldn't say anything because I knew that they were not open to anything outside the medical system. The sad thing is that most of the people that did chemotherapy ended up coming back as the cancer seemed to come back. I would explain that cancer is an acidic condition. It had a lot to do with the diet that they were eating. People find that so hard to believe and yet so simple because the ones that did actually get incredible results were the ones that did both the cannabis and the diet. I was only there to guide them and help support them with their choices.

Soon I opened my own clinic not too far from the clinic where I had been sharing. It was time for me to step out and put together all of the knowledge that I had to support others. I wondered how I would go, but I had been getting so many referrals based on my diet plan that I decided to take the risk. Not only was I getting more referrals, but also people that wanted to study with me. This was something that I was thinking of putting together in the future, a training program to help people educate others on medical cannabis and help them with their diet.

It seemed that doctors just didn't have time to study and go in depth into medical cannabis to help their patients, so they were always very impressed when I was able to teach them about how it worked in the human body. I was getting referrals from all over Australia and even Colorado. I wondered why someone had contacted me from Colorado when cannabis is legal there and I did say to the girl, "Wouldn't there be lots of people doing what I do in Colorado?"

And she said, "No, I haven't found anyone that does what you do with Dr Morse's herbs and educating people on medical cannabis."

Things were definitely better in my life. I realise as I write this last chapter, it's November 26, 2019, the day before my 54th birthday, so it's been exactly 10 years of this topsy-turvy, challenging, up-and-down time for me. I think back to the person that I was 10 years ago and I would hardly recognise her today. I certainly have less attachment to things that are transient. As my experience and having everything ripped from me that was transient had taught me, nothing lasts forever and no one belongs to us and anything can change overnight.

The person I've become is a much stronger woman, stronger on the inside and softer on the outside. I would say that my boundaries are definitely stronger too and that I can now say 'no'. I can put myself first and then take care of others. I now do so from a full cup, not an empty cup. I worked out that people pleasing doesn't serve anyone, not the person you're trying to please or yourself. I worked out that I didn't need to please other people to be enough and feel that I'm making a difference. I finally learned to take care of myself as much as I take care of others. I am very careful about who I spend time with, who I let into my life. If I don't feel good in their presence, I don't spend time with them. I am very careful of any contracts, and still regularly revoke contracts. I realise that I am the creator of my life within a matrix control system and the more I stay in my own sovereignty, the more I can create. I look in the mirror and know that my skin suit is not me. It has more wrinkles, less toned, but as I age, I do so from a very solid place within. I know that there is only a fraction of who I truly am living inside this skin suit and I have access to a much wiser me, who has been trying to guide me all through my life. I have learned to listen to that still voice within. She knows what I need more than anyone outside. I still love to hear experts and healers share their knowledge but know that no one person has all the answers. I take information and filter it through my own being.

My desire to know my spiritual purpose was my fuel over these past 10 years. In the midst of the tears, tantrums and turmoil I was becoming. But I was seeking outside of myself for answers from gurus and teachers and was a lot more gullible. My beliefs have changed so much and

I'm sure they will continue to change as they're also transient, but I know without a doubt that my spiritual purpose is to serve others.

I choose service to humanity and know that's why I came here. That's why I volunteered, you see. As a way shower, a path cutter, a teacher, a helper, and a guide or an angel undercover. To be undercover, we have to forget who we are. Like the photo on my cover, the angel has had her wings removed. I see that as her leaving her wings with God for a while, going through all the painful experiences as a human, to know the human suffering, to live it fully. Then through the suffering, remember who we are. Remember the wings were always there and the warrior angel depicted on the cover photo is revealed to us as our true Self. We all need to find that warrior angel within us. I realise I didn't come here to this life to be a mother or a wife and that's okay if that is your purpose, but it's not mine. I can only be fulfilled when I know that I'm doing my life's purpose and I do so from experience, by going through the challenges, finding a way out and then leaving the path for others. Teaching others how I got there, how I survived, how I grew through the experience and how I finally learned to listen to myself and know my wings were always there and always will be.

The most important lesson of all for me has been realising my Soul created all of this. The people I drew into my sphere, my Soul summoned there. I now believe that all the people who hurt, cheated, lied and betrayed me were my greatest teachers and the psychic attacks could only take place because I consciously or unconsciously agreed to them. Through all of these experiences I received what I needed to be who I am now and without them I would not know mySelf or my strength as I do now. I have no anger in my heart towards any of the 'actors' who played their roles in my life. I truly loved all of them. I am no longer a victim because I know I am the creator of my life.

Collectively, the truth is being revealed. Corruption is being exposed. Paedophiles, the sex trade and the deep state's control over us are all being exposed. We are currently living in the time of The Great

Return to Love and Purpose

Awakening. Where I was asleep in the matrix, thinking from a victim mentality, believing I had no control over my circumstances, we, as the human race, are also in that same mentality. But we are currently waking up to the realisation that our abusers, controllers and the dark forces can only exist because we allow them to.

The dark forces cannot survive without our energy and consent. Just like the narcissist survives on narcissistic supply from his victim, and moves on to another when the empath takes back her power, they will no longer survive, when we as the collective take back ours. Ironically, it's the dark forces that are waking up the sleeping masses. Like actors playing their part on the stage of life, they are playing a part in the awakening of humanity. But only if we wake up to our light within as individuals first. We must stop looking outside for a saviour to fix us and look within at our own darkness. We need to accept, love and forgive ourselves, then we can do so for others. Love is the most powerful force in the universe and that is what will change our world.

There is a saying that one day when you meet the guru on the path, you will kill him. This means that one day you'll no longer need a guru or anything outside yourself because you have become your own guru. The word guru means dispeller of darkness.

I hope, dear reader, in reading this book it has reminded you of why you came to this earth. What is the purpose of your birth? Who did you come to be and are you really being all you can be? Are you an angel undercover? Then perhaps, by reading this book, it will remind you that you do have wings, you always have, you are the light that can make a difference to your own life and the world. The world needs more light. The world needs more renegades. The world needs you!

"Our deepest fear is not that we are inadequate. Our deepest fear is that we are powerful beyond measure. It is our light, not our darkness that most frightens us. We ask ourselves, Who am I to be brilliant, gorgeous, talented, fabulous? Actually, who are you *not* to be? You are a child of God. Your playing small does not serve the world. There is nothing enlightened about shrinking so that other people won't feel insecure around you. We are all meant to shine, as children do. We were born to make manifest the glory of God that is within us. It's not just in some of us; it's in everyone. And as we let our own light shine, we unconsciously give other people permission to do the same. As we are liberated from our own fear, our presence automatically liberates others."

Marianne Williamson

About the Author

Norma Strang was born in Scotland 1965 and moved to Australia in 1987. For the next 33 years her journey has been one of self-discovery where she pursued many different schools of teaching. Her pursuit of happiness and health became her purpose, achieving certifications as a Yoga Instructor, Raw Food Chef, Hypnotherapist, Detoxification Specialist, Medical Cannabis educator and more… Her passion is to share the skills and tools she gained along the way with others.

normastrang.com

Notes

Undercover Angel

Notes

Lightning Source UK Ltd.
Milton Keynes UK
UKHW011453121020
371441UK00001B/79

9 781922 372840